D1266072

Living History
of
Brisbane

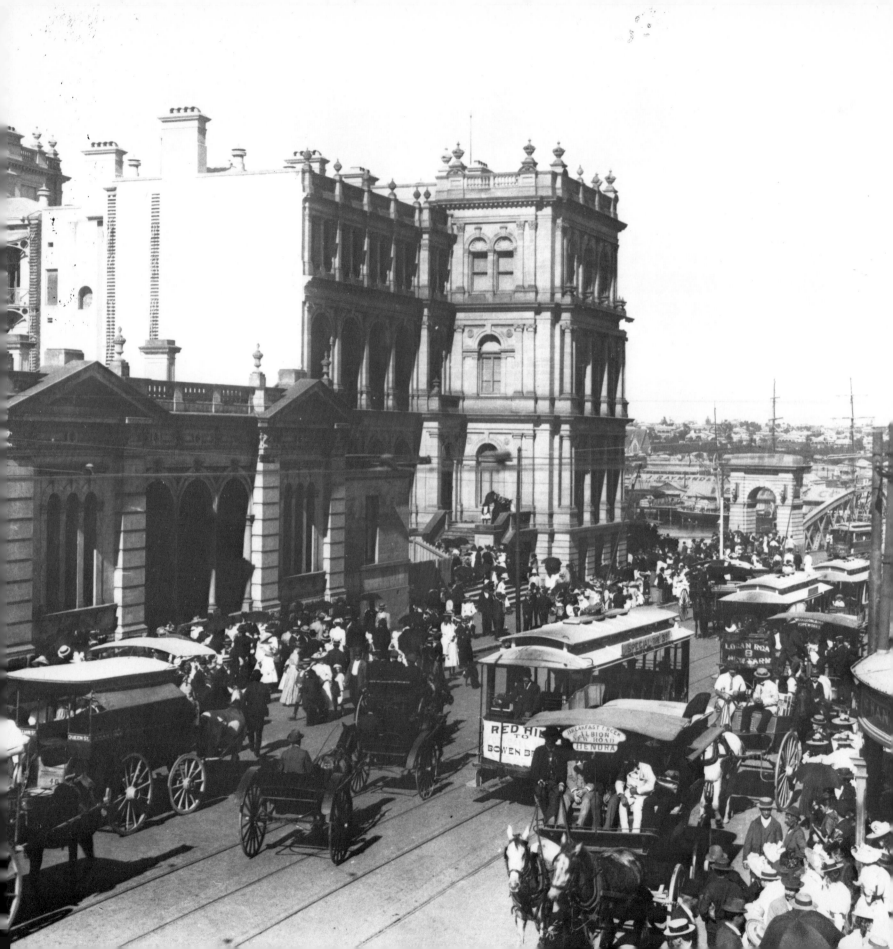

Living History
of
Brisbane

by

Janet Hogan

A BOOLARONG PUBLICATION

First published 1982. Second Edition 1988
by Boolarong Publications,
12 Brookes Street, Bowen Hills, Brisbane. Qld 4006.

National Library of Australia
Cataloguing-in-Publication data.
  Hogan, Janet.
    Living History of Brisbane.

  ISBN 0 908175 41 8.

    1. Brisbane (Qld.) — History.
    I. Title.

994.3'1

BOOLARONG PUBLICATIONS
12 Brookes Street, Bowen Hills, Brisbane. Qld 4006.

Design, reproduction and photo-typesetting
in 11½ on 13 point Baskerville by
Press Etching (Qld) Pty Ltd, Brisbane.

Printed by Apple Printing Co. Pty Ltd, Brisbane.

Bound by Podlich Enterprises Pty Ltd, Brisbane.

Front Cover: *Fireworks light the evening sky at the
conclusion of the celebrations to mark the opening of the
new Queensland Art Gallery, on the south bank of the
Brisbane River, on 21 June 1982.*

Back Cover: *The distant modern city skyline forms a
contrasting backdrop to the Coronation Hotel at South
Brisbane, 1982.*

Frontispiece: *Crowds in Queen Street near the partially
completed Treasury Building and the new Victoria
Bridge, 1897.*

Contents

Acknowledgements

Photography for this book was undertaken by Richard Stringer with the following exceptions:

Cover photo — courtesy State Public Relations Bureau, Premier's Department; Aborigines fishing — courtesy Photographic Unit, Queensland State Archives; School of Arts — courtesy Civic Art Gallery, Brisbane City Council; Woodlands — from the collection of Peter and Adrian Grant; Rhyndarra — courtesy Rhys Beames; Ship Inn, Plough Inn, South Brisbane Municipal Library, Stanley Street 1893, General Douglas MacArthur — courtesy Queensland Newspapers Pty Ltd; Superimposed model of World Expo 88 — courtesy World Expo 88.

Grateful acknowledgement is accorded the following for permission to reproduce works in their collections:

Mitchell Library, Sydney — sketch of Moreton Bay, 1831; Archives Authority of New South Wales — *Plan of a design for a Treadmill adapted for Country Districts*; Queensland Government Department of Mapping and Surveying — Plan of Brisbane Town by Robert Dixon, 24 March 1842; Queensland State Archives and Premier's Department — elevations of the Commissariat Stores and Yungabah Immigration Depot; Queensland Women's Historical Association — servicewomen with kangaroos; National Australia Bank Archives — former Queensland National Bank, Stanley Street, South Brisbane; National Library of Australia —

    Moreton Bay New South Wales 1835
    pencil sketch 22.4 cm × 36.2 cm
    NK 211
    In the Rex Nan Kivell collection
    National Library of Australia.

Other old illustrations, except where cited, have been reproduced by kind permission of the John Oxley Library, for which I am sincerely grateful.

Thanks are due to the many people who gave encouragement to me to write this book and to those who assisted to bring it to its successful fruition, including:

Mr Colin Sheehan (John Oxley Librarian); Mr Paul Wilson (former State Archivist); Ms Lee McGregor (State Archivist); Dr Ruth Kerr, Deputy State Archivist; Mr Ross Fraser (State Public Relations Officer); Mr Brian Breingan (Courier-Mail Librarian); Mr Rhys Beames (former Historic Buildings Liaison Officer, Department of Housing and Construction); Miss Gyneth Campbell (Honorary Secretary, Queensland Women's Historical Association); Mrs Jane Gibson (former Promotions Officer, Queensland Art Gallery); Mr Duncan McDermott (formerly Photographic Section, Brisbane City Council); former and present staff of the John Oxley Library, in particular Mr Robert Longhurst, Miss Mamie O'Keeffe, Ms Noreen Kirkman and Mr John Cook; Mr Sandy Barrie, Ranald Simmonds Studio; Father Frank Moynihan (Administrator, St Stephen's Cathedral); Ms Mary Weaver (State Library of Queensland); Mrs Pamela Whitlock (Curator, Civic Art Gallery); Mrs Patricia Ramsay (Diocesan Archivist, St John's Cathedral); Mr Arthur O'Neill (former Archivist, National Australia Bank); Mr A.R. White (Coopers Plains); Mr Peter Owen, Ms Jane West and Ms Marlene McKendry (World Expo 88).

The assistance of the following as sources of information is acknowledged:

J.G. Steele, *Brisbane Town in Convict Days 1824–1842* (Brisbane, 1975); M. O'Keeffe, *A Brief Account of the Moreton Bay Penal Settlement 1824–1839* (Brisbane, 1974); Cassell's *Picturesque Australasia* (Melbourne, 1887–89); Carolyn Nolan, 'T.C. Beirne' in *Brisbane Retrospect: Eight Aspects of Brisbane History* (Brisbane, 1978); Vera McComb, *A Tribute to the Clarkson and Henry Families of Fig Tree Pocket* (Brisbane, 1970); Percy E. Hunter, *The Brisbane School of Arts Centenary 1849–1949* (Brisbane, 1949).

Finally, I would like to thank my husband, Austin, for his moral support, understanding and encouragement, without which the book could not have been written; Mr Les Padman and Mrs Elaine Bagnall of Boolarong Publications, for their faith in an idea, which made the publication of the book possible; Craig Padman and the staff of Press Etching (Qld) Pty Ltd, for their achievement in production of the book in a short time; and Noel Hobson for his belief that *Living History of Brisbane* is worth promoting in the interests of the conservation of Queensland's heritage.

Preface

The presentation of the historical setting of Brisbane from European settlement to the present day provides a means for better understanding this capital city of Queensland today. The significant features of Brisbane's past directly relating to places or events readily identifiable today have thus been selected for inclusion in *Living History of Brisbane.*

The text links the past to the present and provides a brief explanation, historical or descriptive, relative to the event or place. Contemporary illustrations have been used wherever possible to place the feature in its original setting and to create an awareness of the importance of old photographs and other records, thereby stimulating their retention in the State Collection in the John Oxley Library, or by other similar bodies. Much of this material is presently being lost to posterity through a lack of understanding of its historical and research value.

Many of the places included in this book are listed by The National Trust of Queensland and others are awaiting consideration. The history of a city is written in its buildings, the physical evidence left by those people who have shaped our history and will continue to do so into the future. By creating a better understanding of Brisbane's built environment, this book aims to help in the preservation of those places which are of particular significance to our heritage.

British architect Ian Grant, in a report to Unesco in 1972, said that ''man's understanding of the value of the products of the past is a relatively new expression of his progress in civilization, in comparison with the length of time that he has left the barbaric state behind him. The desire to preserve those products as an inspiration to future generations, in the chain of continuity which every healthy culture requires, is even newer still''.

Living History of Brisbane is concerned with the promotion of this understanding of the past and present for the future — through our better understanding of the historic places and events significant to the capital today, such things have an increased chance of survival into the future to continue Brisbane's 'living history'.

Major-General Sir Thomas Macdougall Brisbane and Settlement

When Britain established a penal settlement at Sydney Cove in 1788, the area now comprising Brisbane was part of the colony of New South Wales. In 1819 Commissioner Bigge was sent from England to report generally on the state of the colony, and he recommended that several penal settlements should be established around the coast as places of secondary punishment, to which persons already serving sentences of transportation could be sent after further convictions.

In 1823 the Surveyor-General, John Oxley, explored the Moreton Bay area and recommended it as suitable for the establishment of a penal settlement. He also named the Brisbane River in honour of the Governor of New South Wales from 1821 to 1825, Major-General Sir Thomas Macdougall Brisbane.

Though suggestions were made in London that the area might be preferable for free settlement, Governor Brisbane proceeded with his plans for a convict settlement, believing that 'the Establishment of Penal Depots is the best means of paving the way for the introduction of free population'. He envisaged Moreton Bay as a place for minor offenders who had been sentenced to relatively short terms.

In September 1824 a settlement was established at Redcliffe, on the shores of Moreton Bay, but during the first half of 1825 the settlement was relocated to the banks of the Brisbane River — the present site of Brisbane's William Street and the southern end of Queen Street.

Governor Brisbane's instructions to the Commandant of the new penal settlement stated that

> Your first attention immediately on arrival, is to be directed to the Choice of an airy Situation, contiguous to fresh Water, for the Site of your Encampment. — Not a moment is then to be lost in constructing huts for the Soldiers and Convicts. — Those for the Troops are to be placed in a commanding situation, three hundred yards distant from the huts intended for the others. — The former should be enclosed by a strong palisade and ditch, to secure them from Assault. As soon as this has been effected, a Store, a Guard House, and a Gaol ought to be erected. — These Buildings complete you are to employ all your Force to clear and prepare, for the reception of Maize, One hundred Acres of the best Soil near the Settlement. — It being intended that the new Establishment shall, within a short space of Time, subsist entirely on its resources . . .

> The Ration to be issued to each Convict is to consist of four Pounds of Salt Meat and   pounds of Flour, but you will be entitled yourself to draw a treble allowance. The hours of Morning Labour will be from day light till eight, when one hour and a half will be given for cleanliness and breakfast. Work will be resumed from half past nine until twelve. Two hours will then be allowed for Dinner, and Labour will afterwards continue from 2 O'Clock until Sunset. — On Sunday Mornings the Convicts are to bath and when perfectly clean to be mustered for Divine Service, which is to be performed by yourself.

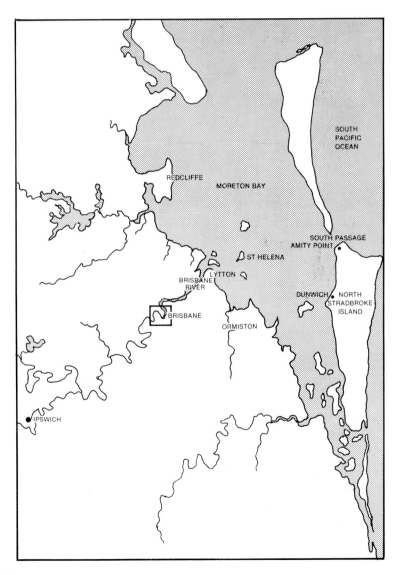

Above: *King Jackie of the Enoggera Tribe with his gin and daughter outside their 'gunyah'. An Aboriginal 'dilly' hangs above King Jackie's head, but the tin cans (or 'billies') in the foreground and King Jackie's breast-plate are subtle indications of the influence of British settlement.*

Opposite: *Aborigines fishing. The creeks and waterholes, such as Breakfast Creek, Enoggera Creek and Kedron Brook, provided a plentiful food supply for the Aborigines in the Brisbane area.*

Settlement and the Aborigines

Before setting out for Moreton Bay, the first commandant received instructions from Governor Brisbane regarding the local Aborigines, which stated that 'You will take an early opportunity of establishing a friendly intercourse with the neighbouring Blacks, but you will not admit them to an imprudent familiarity — Whenever they apprehend stray Cattle or runaways small presents are to be issued to them of food, tomahawks, or fish hooks and you are to punish severely any ill-treatment of them . . .'.

Further instructions followed two days later. 'In order to insure an amicable understanding with the Black Natives, good faith must ever be your guide, in your public dealings with them. Private injuries towards them must be repressed

with care; and if a public or private wrong cannot be avenged by law, it must be repaired by compensation to the sufferers. All uncivilized people have wants, which can be cheaply and honorably gratified by us; and when treated justly, they acquire many comforts by their union with the more civilized. This justifies our occupation of their lands. It should be your chief object therefore to cause justice to be done, on all possible occasions; and when you may happen not to be able to remove all the occasions of differences, this unavoidable evil should be lessened by increased liberality . . .'.

The Aborigines were grouped together into small tribes, each belonging to a certain locality. They were constantly on the move and their 'gunyah', or primitive hut, was easily made from readily available materials such as sticks and tree bark. A small bag or 'dilly' was used for carrying food and other property, such as 'their most formidable weapon' — a stone knife or blade of steel. Their water utensils were made from either wood or the large leaf of a banana-like plant.

The food source of the Aborigines was both animal and vegetable. Christopher Eipper, a member of the German Mission to the Aborigines established at Moreton Bay towards the end of the convict period, said that 'more than half of their time every day is taken up in procuring their food and . . . if not engaged in procuring food, they employ themselves either in repairing their nets, sharpening their spears, carving their waddies, or making new ones; or they will idle away their time in chatting, and other playful amusements . . . The nights are . . . taken up with dancing and singing . . .'.

A pencil sketch of the penal settlement at Moreton bay in 1831 (from the Mitchell Library Collection). This view from South Brisbane towards what is now North Quay shows the only convict buildings existing today — the Windmill (top left) and the Commissariat Store (bottom right). Both buildings were begun in 1828.

Brisbane in the 1830s

Buildings initially were temporary, 'constructed of slabs and plastering for want of proper mechanics to erect others'. But as the population grew, larger buildings of brick and stone were erected. Of these, only two remain today — the former Windmill on Wickham Terrace and the former Commissariat Store in William Street. It was during the period when Captain Patrick Logan was Commandant (March 1826 to October 1830) that the period of building expansion was greatest. Logan was murdered by Aborigines near Brisbane in October 1830, just prior to his planned departure from Moreton Bay.

Despite Governor Brisbane's initial instructions that 'the new Establishment shall, within a short space of Time, subsist entirely on its resources', as late as December 1827 the lack of any means of grinding grain at Brisbane was

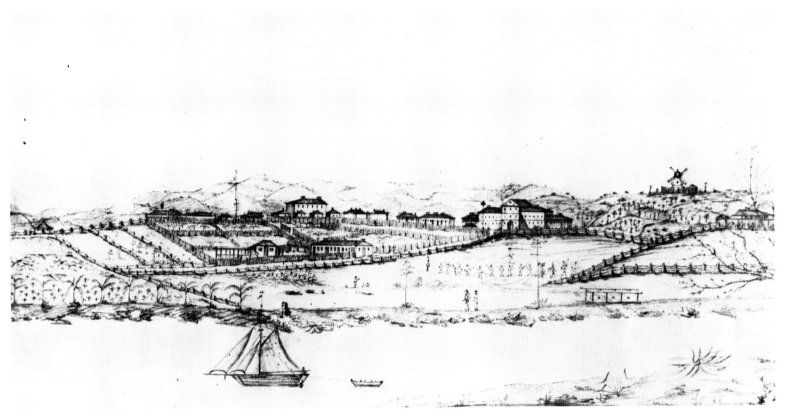

The penal settlement sketched from Kangaroo Point in 1835 (from the Rex Nan Kivell Collection, National Library of Australia). The Female Factory, where the female prisoners lived and worked, is at the right; the Convict Barracks building, where male prisoners were accommodated, is towards the centre; and the Military Barracks complex (for the soldiers) is also near the centre of the picture. All three sites line present day Queen Street.

discussed in correspondence between officials in Brisbane and Sydney. On 6 June 1828 the Colonial Secretary Alexander McLeay advised Captain Logan that 'as the numbers on the settlement will be materially increased within a short period, you will be pleased to take steps for extending the land in cultivation, it being important on every account that the government should be relieved from the trouble and expense of sending supplies of this nature from hence'. A mill was begun on a hill above the settlement in July 1828 and was in operation by the following October.

Before construction of the mill, flour in casks was shipped to the settlement from Sydney. With the introduction of local grinding facilities, locally grown wheat and maize could be utilized or wheat in bags could be conveyed from Sydney when necessary — the latter was more conveniently stored and occupied less room in a vessel's hold than did flour in casks.

Maize, corn in cobs, and wheat were taken by the convicts in a hand cart from the fields to a barn near the corner of present day Albert and Elizabeth Streets. Here, thrashing was carried out by the prisoners and the grain was then carried by bullock dray or handcart from the barn to the Windmill, along the route visible in the picture.

The convicts at Brisbane were guarded by soldiers from British regiments on station in New South Wales and there were usually about 100 soldiers at the settlement. The number of convicts at Brisbane reached a peak of 947 in 1831, but by 1835 the number had dropped to 374.

By 1831 agriculture was well established, the settlement was self-supporting, and out-stations had been established at Eagle Farm (agriculture), Ipswich (limestone), Dunwich (stores) and Amity Point (pilot station).

Above: *A chain gang — convicts going to work, c 1836. (Reproduced from James Backhouse, **A narrative of a visit to the Australian Colonies,** 1843).*

Top right: *This enlargement of part of the sketch on page 13 shows the convicts working under supervision in the fields; the track leading from the settlement to Windmill Hill; the Female Factory (right); and the Convict Barracks — the largest building in the settlement.*

Bottom right: *The Windmill, Queensland's first industrial building and its oldest building extant, stands on the hill above the settlement where it can take advantage of prevailing breezes. It is possible that the structure to the left of the Windmill is the Treadmill. (Enlargement of part of the sketch on page 12).*

The Windmill

The Windmill was a tower mill of four floors and contained two pair of mill stones — one pair connected to the windmill and one pair connected by a shaft to a treadmill outside. The tower was constructed of stone and brick and the sails were tended by means of a perimeter platform about one third of the way up the tower.

From the diary of Peter Beauclerk Spicer, Superintendent of Convicts from September 1826 to May 1839, we learn that on Friday, 25 July 1828, 8 convicts began clearing ground for the foundations of a Mill. On 28 July, 17 convicts began digging foundations and on Friday, 31 October, 26 convicts forming a Mill Gang were employed grinding wheat — the first known record of such an event in Brisbane. A Mill Gang continued grinding wheat until 15 December 1828, and during this time some of the convicts were also employed thrashing and cleaning wheat.

There seems little doubt from available evidence that the

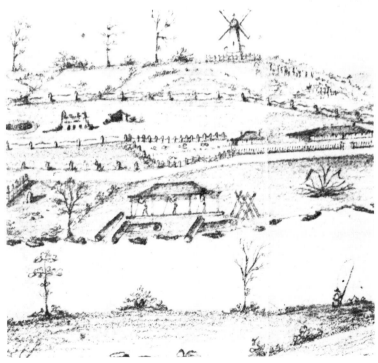

Windmill was built in 1828 and is the oldest surviving building in Queensland. Due to lack of servicing and maintenance by experienced persons, the Windmill was subject to periodic breakdown and when this occurred it was usually necessary to obtain from Sydney someone with a knowledge of Windmills — 'a volunteer prisoner if such can be found of sufficient skill'.

By January 1836 the Windmill was in a 'near perfect state', but within a month the mill was struck by lightning. George Webb, a prisoner in Sydney who was a millwright, volunteered to repair the Mill and on 28 May 1837 the Commandant reported that Webb had repaired the mills which were now 'equal to any in the colony and very valuable'.

After the closure of the Penal Settlement in 1839, the Windmill continued in use, supplying food for those preparing for the opening up of Moreton Bay to free settlement. Subsequently, the mill fell into disuse and it was converted to a Signal Station in 1861.

The Treadmill

Whether the Treadmill was erected contemporaneously with the Windmill is unclear — there was no Treadmill at Brisbane in December 1827, but in September 1829 a prisoner lost his life 'by becoming entangled in the Tread wheel'. The Treadmill was used when the Windmill was being repaired, in calm weather, or as a means of punishment. George Washington Walker, one of the two Quaker missionaries who were permitted to visit the settlement in March 1836, recorded his impressions of the Treadmill, which were published in 1862 in *The life and labours of George Washington Walker of Hobart Town.*

Went into the yard where the chain gang, consisting of twenty five men, were at work on the tread-wheel. These are so employed because the power is wanted, not because it is a part of their sentence; therefore they are not so hard worked as if

Below and Opposite: *The Colonial Architect's plans for the 'Design for Tread Mill Adapted for Country Districts. Average Estimate £120' (Archives Authority of New South Wales). Brisbane's Treadmill may have been constructed to or based on this design.*

Far right: *George Washington Walker, a Quaker missionary who visited the penal settlement at Moreton Bay in 1836 in company with James Backhouse. Both men left interesting descriptions of the penal settlement which are now valuable historical records.*

they had subjected themselves to this species of discipline as an extra punishment. In that case they work from sunrise to sunset, with a rest of three hours in the middle of the day, in the hot weather, and two hours during the cooler months. There is also a relief of four men, sixteen being constantly on the wheel, which, of course, affords each man an interval of periodical rest, throughout the day, of one-fifth of the whole time, or of one quarter of an hour's rest after every hour of labour. The exertion requisite to keep this up is excessive. I am told the steps of the wheel are sometimes literally wet with the perspiration that drops from the partially naked men; for they generally strip to the waist. It necessarily bears hardest upon those who have been least accustomed to the labour, particularly the men who are the heaviest in person. The Constable who was superintending, told me that the wheel performed 160 revolutions before each man's turn of rest came, which multiplied by 24, the number of steps in the wheel, gives 3840 times each man must lift his feet in continued succession. Any one who has tried the effect of ascending a hundred steps at a time, may form some idea of the excessive exertion this kind of labour involves, though, doubtless, something must be abated on account of the weight with which the men rest with their arms or hands on the cross rail.

Punishment by the Treadmill was given for such offences as 'insolence and disgusting language', 'gross insubordination', 'grumbling about the Mill going too fast', 'jumping on the Mill Wheel with the intention of doing it an injury', and stealing maize meal.

No specific plans have been located for the erection of either the Windmill or the Treadmill. The Archives Authority of New South Wales holds plans by the Colonial Architect for a 'Design for Tread Mill Adapted for Country Districts Average Estimate £120'. It is possible that treadmills at the various penal establishments, including Moreton Bay, were constructed to or based on this design. Indeed, when the Commandant of Norfolk Island in 1831 requested a treadmill that could be 'appropriated as a punishment as well as to the grinding of grain', instructions were given 'to furnish the usual plans and estimates'.

The Treadmill, located outside the Windmill and connected to it by a shaft, was detached from the Windmill sometime prior to October 1849. It has been postulated recently, using old maps, that the Treadmill may have been located towards either Wickham Park or Wickham Terrace.

The Commissariat Store

The second oldest building extant in Brisbane, the Commissariat Store was built between May 1828 and the end of 1829, and was one of the major works begun during Captain Logan's period as Commandant. It was a two storey building with hammer-dressed coarse freestone walls, corner stones of Brisbane tuff or porphyry, and floors supported by bearers of ironbark 9 m long and .3 m square. This was the second Commissariat Store erected at the penal settlement and the upper storey was to be used as a granary.

After the closure of the penal settlement, the Commissariat Store was used to house immigrants, initially accommodating the overflow from the nearby depot on the present Treasury Building site and later acting as the Immigration Depot. More recently it was used by the Queensland State Archives and the Law Reform Commission, and it is now occupied (after renovation) as the headquarters of the Royal Historical Society of Queensland.

Many additions and alterations have been made to the building over the years. In 1886 a single storey brick

structure was added as a south-eastern wing, to which a second storey was added in 1900. During recent renovations this wing was demolished to reveal the entire existing main facade of the original Commissariat Store. A third storey of brickwork was added to the original building in 1912–13. Recently, the roof of this main three storey structure has been raised and covered with slates, and the building has been adapted internally for re-use by its present occupants.

Top left: *The Commissariat Store today. The third storey was added to the original stone building in 1912–13.*

Bottom Left: *Elevation of the Commissariat Store at Moreton Bay, begun in 1828 and completed in 1829. (From Plan 17, Moreton Bay Plans, Queensland State Archives).*

Above: *A small, single storey structure built by the convicts was used as Brisbane's General Post Office in the 1860s. A similar building, which housed the convict settlement's solitary cells, abutted the G.P.O. to the north. The site of both buildings is now occupied by a Roger David Store (menswear).*

First General Post Office

During Brisbane's convict period, communication with the outside world was by mail which came and went by sea. Even the convicts were allowed to send and receive mail — but only after scrutiny by the Commandant. Thus the job of 'postmaster' existed from the very early convict days. When Brisbane was opened up to free settlement the postmaster, who was also the Commandant's Clerk, lived in Queen Street in the residence of the former Superintendent of Convicts, Peter Beauclerk Spicer, who had returned to Sydney. This is marked as the post office in maps of Brisbane at this time.

Photos from the late 1860s show the G.P.O. in a convict built structure which seems to have had a varied career as a married soldiers' quarters, a military school, and a kitchen and an office for Spicer, whose residence was next door. The adjacent building on the other (northern) side was used as solitary cells, built about 1827–29. Bribane's first Town Hall was built next door. The former cells and adjacent Post Office were demolished for the construction of the Colonial Mutual Life Assurance Society's Brisbane headquarters in 1883 (now occupied by a menswear store).

Brisbane, c 1840.

'Humpy' on Zion's Hill, said to be a cottage of one of the German missionary families, c 1870.

Brisbane Prepared for Free Settlement

The average number of convicts at Moreton Bay reached a peak of 947 in 1831. In 1832 serious consideration was given to the closing down of the penal settlement, and though this was postponed, numbers were reduced from that time. In May 1839 most of the remaining convicts were returned to Sydney and the numbers of officials and of the military were also reduced. By November 1839 there were only 29 prisoners under colonial sentence still at Moreton Bay and these attended to the work of the settlement which was now in a transition period, being surveyed in preparation for free settlement.

The order proclaiming the Moreton Bay area a penal settlement was rescinded on 11 February 1842 and thereafter 'all settlers and other free persons shall be at liberty to proceed thither in like manner as to any other part of the colony'. During Moreton Bay's penal settlement days, any person not connected with the settlement was forbidden to come within fifty miles of it. At the same time it was announced that the first building allotments in Brisbane would be sold by auction in Sydney 'as soon after the first day of July next as the necessary preparatory arrangements . . . can be completed'.

German Mission to the Aborigines at Moreton Bay

A German Mission, approved by the government, was established a few kilometres from the main penal settlement in 1838. Named Zion's Hill, the site is now part of the suburb of Nundah. Writing in 1841 in the *Statement of the Origin, Conditions and Prospects of the German Mission to the Aborigines at Moreton Bay* Christopher Eipper, one of the missionaries, said that 'The Missionary Settlement is situated seven miles northward from Brisbane town, and about two miles north-west from Eagle farm, now a Government cattle station, but formerly an agricultural settlement and Female Factory. It is, from its situation, peculiarly adapted for missionary exertions, as it lies at the great thoroughfare of the Aborigines, when proceeding either from the north or south along the sea-coast, as well as of those coming from the interior; and it may safely be said, that nowhere are there so many natives met with together as at Moreton Bay, which makes it as important a locality for a mission, as it is in other respects a favourable one.

'The number of aborigines in the district is not easily ascertained, as the occasions are rare on which they assemble in great numbers. At fights, which have taken place in the neighbourhood of the settlement, and even of the missionary station, as many as from 200 to 300 have been present'.

On the settlement itself, the Reverend Eipper wrote that 'the labours of the missionaries have hitherto, from sheer necessity, been confined in great measure to the preliminary operations of clearing ground, erecting houses, and other buildings, and fencing in, and breaking up ground for cultivation. Their settlement is situated on a hill; . . . it consists of eleven cottages with inclosed yards, kitchens, storehouses etc.: these cottages are built in a line on the ridge of the hill . . . The houses are either thatched or covered with bark; the walls are built with slabs and plastered with clay both inside and outside, being whitewashed with a species of white clay found on the spot, and mixed with sand. The ceilings are formed of plaits of grass and clay wound about sticks laid across the tie-beams, and the floors of slabs smoothed with the adze; each cottage having two or three rooms and one fire place . . .

'The only means of conveyance from the Settlement to the Mission Station, excepting the occasional loan of a dray granted to the missionaries through the kindness of the Government Officers, has been the shoulders of the Missionaries: and the only means of bringing this land into cultivation, as well as of getting a cover over their heads, was the labour of their own hands. When it is considered therefore that they had never been accustomed to bushwork, that they were destitute of materials suitable for building — tools not excepted — till they had formed them themselves by their manual labour, it will doubtless be allowed that enough has been done, at all events, to exempt them from the reproach of idleness.'

Many of the missionaries and their families are buried in the Nundah Cemetery in Hedley Avenue, which dates from the days of early settlement by the German missionaries.

A view in the Nundah Cemetery where many of the German missionaries and their families are buried.

The causeway at Dunwich was built by convict labour but has been added to in recent years.

Aboriginal graves on Stradbroke Island.

Dunwich

The early shipping route to Brisbane was via South Passage, past Amity Point and Dunwich on Stradbroke Island. To eliminate the journey up the river to Brisbane, a stores depot and military post were established at Dunwich in 1827 for vessels visiting the bay to take in and discharge cargo. However, it was found that in rough weather cargoes were lost and that the Aborigines on the island were hostile, so the settlement was discontinued after about 1831. The original stone causeway erected by the convicts at Dunwich still exists, though it has been modified and enlarged to accommodate the larger ships and heavy vehicles associated with the local mineral sands industry. After the *Sovereign* was wrecked in 1847 whilst crossing the South Passage bar and 40 lives were lost, the northern entrance to Moreton Bay became the normal shipping route from 1848.

*Queensland's first immigrant ship, the **Artemisia**, reached Moreton Bay in December 1848.*

First Immigrant Ship

Increased exploration of the inland areas opened up more of the country and as settlement spread, the ships bringing in supplies and settlers and taking away produce increased in numbers.

Progress of settlement, however, was hampered by a lack of suitable supporting labour, such as manual workers, tradesmen and domestics. In response to this demand the first immigrant ship, the *Artemisia*, carrying over 200 immigrants, left England for Moreton Bay in August 1848 and arrived in Brisbane in December. Her departure was described in the *Illustrated London News* on 12 August 1848:

It was curious to note how unconscious the children appeared of their new position, or rather how soon they had become accustomed to it. All save these seemed to be hard workers; many, who had scarcely reached manhood, bore the strong lines of care on their faces; and any one who had not been apprised of the conditions on which they obtained their passage would have set them down among the industrious classes.

We now inspected the accommodation between decks where a number of the passengers were seated — some playing with their children, others reading, and here and there might be seen one whose thoughtful air rather denoted sorrow . . . We were glad to find so many books in hand; what a friend must a huge entertaining volume be upon a long voyage! We were happy also to see the officers of the Prayer book and the Homily Society distributing their publications: what hopes must they nourish, in time of peril upon the waters! By and by came the dinner — the meat well cooked and of good quality; though, of course, the table had not all the snugness of the cottage meal. The parties were in messes of six or eight individuals and the comfort of the voyage is much studied by berthing near each other those who come from the same part of the country and messing as nearly as possible those who are friends. The great order maintained on board is also indicated by the "Regulations" and "Dietary Scales" hung up in conspicuous places between decks . . .

Towards evening the *Artemisia* made ready to sail: our Artist has represented the fine ship getting under way, fore-topsails set, heaving up anchor, etc. She was next taken in tow by a steam tug to Gravesend: we proceeded in her a short distance, and there, with heartiest wishes for a safe voyage, we bade adieu to the new ship, freighted with so many anxious souls.

Immigrants on board the **Artemisia**.

Hazards of Early Settlement

With the increasing numbers of immigrants arriving at Moreton Bay, the New South Wales quarantine regulations were extended to Moreton Bay which was then still part of that colony. Because of its proximity to the shipping route, its isolation and its adequate supply of fresh water, the northern end of Stradbroke Island was proclaimed a quarantine station on 16 July 1850.

Within a month the ship *Emigrant* arrived in the bay with typhus raging on board. The *Emigrant* was quarantined at Dunwich and temporary accommodation was provided by a dozen worn tents from Brisbane and makeshift shelters constructed from ships parts. Those who died from the disease included the ship's surgeon, 26 immigrants and a Brisbane resident, Dr David Keith Ballow, who undertook to tend the sick after the ship's doctor had died and another local doctor had fallen victim to the disease. These typhus victims were buried at Dunwich and their graves are preserved in the Dunwich cemetery as a silent reminder of the hazards of early settlement.

Above: *Graves of typhus victims from the ship* **Emigrant***, who were quarantined at Dunwich on Stradbroke Island in 1850. A local doctor, David Keith Ballow, who died after voluntarily tending the sick, is also buried there. His efforts are commemorated by Ballow Chambers on Wickham Terrace, Brisbane, where many of the local specialist medical fraternity practise.*

Opposite: *This well known illustration of the first house in Brisbane was featured in* **Picturesque Australasia** *in 1887, when the house still survived in George Street.*

First House in Brisbane

The arrival of free settlers heralded vast changes in the appearance of Brisbane. The settlers required accommodation quickly and the earliest houses were small and inexpensive, constructed of readily obtainable materials and in a simple easy-to-put-together style.

'The first private residence built in Brisbane was erected by Captain Coley, a seafaring man, who after separation was appointed usher of the black rod in the legislative council. This modest structure still stood in 1887 in George Street, a humble weatherboard, low-ceilinged cottage, the shingled roof partly covered with creepers'.

Captain Coley's house was typical of many of Brisbane's early dwellings, which were built on small allotments located close to the centre of the settlement. Eventually, however, new homes erected by the settlers came to reflect the extent of their success in this new land and large ornate homes set in spacious grounds soon became a familiar site in what is now suburban Brisbane.

The dwellings erected close to the centre of the settlement in its early days, including Captain Coley's house, have been demolished progressively over the years during redevelopment of what is now Brisbane's inner city area.

Newstead House

Patrick Leslie, one of the first squatters on the Darling Downs, erected Newstead House in 1845–46 overlooking the Brisbane River at the mouth of Breakfast Creek. It is constructed of plastered brick on stone foundations and has a slate roof. Leslie sold Newstead in 1847 to Captain John Clements Wickham, who was Police Magistrate at Moreton Bay and who became Government Resident in 1857. Wickham altered and enlarged Newstead to suit the entertaining befitting the status of such a leading citizen and he established Newstead's reputation as a gay social centre — the scene of lavish entertainment and grand hospitality. After deciding to return overseas, where he died in 1864,

Wickham sold Newstead House which subsequently passed through numerous owners and tenants. The house has been refurbished as a residence by the Friends of Newstead, under the auspices of the Board of Trustees constituted in 1940, to educate people in the life styles of the nineteenth century.

Top left: *A view from Hamilton (c 1870s) showing what is now Kingsford-Smith Drive in the foreground and Newstead House on a rise overlooking the Brisbane River and Breakfast Creek. The surrounding area is now the suburb of Newstead.*

Bottom left: *Newstead House, the oldest house extant in Brisbane, is surrounded by wide verandahs with decorative balustrades.*

Above: *Bulimba House today.*

Bulimba House

In 1849–50 Bulimba House was erected on the banks of the Brisbane River, opposite Newstead House. The two storey stone building was constructed as the town house of Englishman David Cannon McConnel, who owned Cressbrook Station in the Brisbane Valley. Visually resembling a residence of McConnel's homeland, there were nevertheless practical concessions to the local climate, such as a large blank wall facing the western sun and the wide verandahs to the north and south. Sun hoods were added later for further protection from the weather. The suburb of Bulimba developed around the house which has remained as a private residence to this day. *Bulimba* is an Aboriginal word meaning 'place of the magpie lark'.

Wolston House

Wolston House was built in 1852–53 for Dr Stephen Simpson, first Commissioner for Crown Lands at Moreton Bay, and for some time Acting Police Magistrate and Acting Colonial Surgeon. It is a simple, rectangular, gabled farmhouse, constructed of brick and sandstone, and situated on a rise overlooking the junction of the Brisbane River and Wolston Creek. After Simpson returned to England, where he died in 1869, Wolston had a variety of owners until it became the first property acquired by the National Trust of Queensland. It is now open for public inspection.

Above: *Wolston House at Wacol was built as a simple, low-set farmhouse overlooking the Brisbane River. The section at the right of the photo, believed to be a later addition, was demolished some years ago.*

Opposite: *Queen Street in 1858, looking south from the Edward Street intersection. The former Convict Barracks building at the top of Queen Street still dominates the townscape. The Oxford Hotel is under construction at the centre of the picture.*

Separation of the Colony of Queensland

A census taken in 1845 showed that there were 1599 persons in the Moreton Bay and Darling Downs districts; by 1859 what was to become Queensland had a population of 23 520. The town of Brisbane was gradually developing as a leading port — it became a Port of Entry in 1846 and a warehousing port in 1849. In 1850 a Customs House was erected and in the same year the first bank opened in Brisbane.

As the new settlement became established, thoughts of separation from New South Wales began. Gradually the campaign for a new colony strengthened and on 6 June 1859

letters patent creating the new colony of Queensland were issued.

Queensland's first Governor, Sir George Ferguson Bowen, arrived in Brisbane in December 1859 and, in his own words, he found himself in the position of 'an autocrat; the sole source of authority here, without a single soldier and without a single shilling'.

Bowen appointed an interim government until an election could be held, after which the first Parliament met in the former Convict Barracks building in Queen Street, on 22 May 1860. There were two houses, a Legislative Assembly of 26 elected members and a Legislative Council, the Upper House, of 15 members appointed by the Governor.

Brisbane c 1870, showing the Governor's first residence (now the Deanery) at the centre of the picture, on the hill overlooking the river.

The Governor's First Residence

Governor Bowen initially resided in Adelaide House, now the Deanery of Saint John's Cathedral in Ann Street, which was rented for him by the Government until the new official Government House was ready for occupation in 1862. Adelaide House was described at that time as 'the best house in Brisbane town' and was a two storey porphyry and sandstone residence with attics and timber verandahs, which stood on a hill sloping down to the Brisbane River. The main entrance overlooked the river and it was from the balcony above, on 10 December 1859, that the newly arrived Governor read the proclamation establishing Queensland as a separate colony from New South Wales. The hillslope, where the people of Brisbane gathered to listen to Governor Bowen reading the proclamation, was excavated some years later for the smooth continuation of Adelaide Street. The Governor's former residence now stands above a steep cliff and no longer can be approached directly by the main entrance.

Adelaide House was erected in the mid-1850s as the private residence of Dr Hobbs, who arrived in Brisbane in 1849 as surgeon aboard Dr John Dunmore Lang's second immigrant ship, the *Chasley*.

A view from Kangaroo Point showing Government House, George Street (right) and nearby Parliament House (left) with Wickham Terrace and the Windmill (far left) overlooking the settlement.

Government House, George Street

In 1860 construction began on the new official residence for the Governor — on land previously marked out for sale as Township Allotments, until the Brisbane residents successfully petitioned the Government in Sydney to reserve the area 'to build a town Government House upon'.

The Governor first occupied his new residence early in 1862 and he promptly wrote to the Duke of Newcastle that it was 'beautifully situated on a promontory surrounded on three sides by the river Brisbane . . . It stands in the middle of a private domain of about thirty acres and is further separated from the city of Brisbane by the Botanic Gardens . . . and by a public promenade called ''The Queen's

The drawing room at Government House, George Street (1908).

Park''. Beside good public reception rooms, and private apartments for the Governor and his family, the Government House contains also the Executive Council Chamber and offices for the Private Secretary, etc.'.

The building was constructed of sandstone, with the rear portions of Brisbane tuff or porphyry, and included an entrance vestibule, entrance hall, drawing room, morning room, dining room, library, nine bedrooms, dressing room, sitting room or a tenth bedroom, quarters for the A.D.C. and bedrooms for servants.

Additions to the building since 1862 have included a kitchen and ancillary buildings at the rear in 1872; a covered balcony on the first floor, to the north-east, in 1873; the main entrance portico or porte cochère in 1878; and the billiard room of Helidon sandstone, to the north-west, in 1899.

Even the first official Government House wasn't exempt from deficiencies. In 1895 the Government Architect reported that the Governor had drawn his attention to the fact that 'he had no Map Room or Private Office. The room he occupied as an office being also his Library, the room in which he received visitors, and was also used for meetings of the Executive Council'. Problems were also encountered with arrangements for balls at Government House and the

The main entrance vestibule and hall at Government House, George Street (1908).

Government Architect reported in 1896 that 'a great want in connection with Government House is a suitable ballroom, as apart from the inconvenience felt during the time that the principal rooms are dismantled, the frequent removal and replacing of carpets and furniture tends to depreciate their value, and owing to careless handling by workmen employed there is considerable risk of injury to the more delicate and valuable articles as well as to the walls and joinery of the building'.

Government House was extensively renovated and redecorated in 1895–96 and it is possible that much of the furnishing in the only known photos of the interiors of the residence, taken in 1908, was acquired at this time.

In December 1909 the Governor's residence was dedicated for University purposes, but the Governor remained here until July 1910 when he moved to Fernberg, the present Government House. The Governor's billiard room subsequently became the University of Queensland's Senate Room. The University later moved to its present site at Saint Lucia and the former Government House was occupied by the Queensland Institute of Technology (on whose campus it is located). It is now occupied as the headquarters of The National Trust of Queensland and is being renovated by the State Works Department.

Brisbane in 1862

In the early years of free settlement, the former Convict Barracks building was used as the first Supreme Court and first Parliament House, and survived until about 1881–82 when the present buildings on the site were erected (approximately Sportsgirl–Myers). Begun in 1827 and constructed of stone, the building was erected on the western side of Queen Street and extended from near present day Albert Street to about half way along the block towards George Street. It was the largest building in the settlement and when Brisbane was surveyed prior to free settlement it determined the position of Queen Street and the layout of other streets around it.

The Military Barracks complex, erected about 1830–31, survived until the 1880s when it was demolished for construction of the present Treasury Building. It included a central soldiers' barrack flanked by a guard house and the officers' quarters, and the buildings were designed to

Above: *View across the centre of the settlement in 1862. The intersection of Adelaide and Albert Streets is at the left, and the site of the present City Hall and Square is in the foreground. The former Convict Barracks building is at the centre left and the former Military Barracks is near the river towards the centre of the picture. Across the river is South Brisbane.*

Opposite: *Another view from Wickham Terrace in 1862, looking down Edward Street. The former Female Factory compound, on the site of the present G.P.O. in Queen Street, is at the centre of the picture, with St Stephen's Church to the rear across Elizabeth Street. Kangaroo Point is across the river.*

accommodate 'two subaltern officers, four sergeants and one hundred rank and file'. The complex subsequently housed the early immigrants arriving in Brisbane.

Opposite the Military Barracks, across Elizabeth Street, stood St John's Pro-Cathedral erected in 1854. A tablet in Queen's Park today marks the former location of the altar of the church, demolished in 1904 to allow development of the Executive Gardens (now part of Queen's Park), adjacent to the newly constructed Executive Building (now the Land Administration Building).

A swampy area near the centre of the settlement, close to the intersection of Adelaide and Albert Streets, remained vacant for many years. It is now the site of the Brisbane City Hall and City Square.

The former Female Factory, a prison for women, stood on a hill above Queen Street and when the building was later used as a gaol, the site became known as Gaol Hill. The complex was demolished and the ground levelled in the early 1870s, for the erection of the present G.P.O. building. Initially, female prisoners were not sent to Moreton Bay to serve their sentences, but as the number of females arriving in Brisbane increased the Female Factory was erected in about 1828–29. It was a single storey building, surrounded later by a wall 'to prevent unauthorised entry'. The female convicts lived and worked here, their work including needle-work and washing. The women were moved from here to Eagle Farm in 1837. The former Female Factory compound was used as the location for the annual distribution of blankets to the Aborigines on Queen Victoria's birthday.

St Stephens Church, which still stands in Elizabeth Street, was erected in 1850 opposite the rear of the former Female Factory. On the corner of Edward and Adelaide Streets, on the site now occupied by the State Government building housing the Queensland Government Travel Centre, the Normal School was under construction in 1862. This building was demolished in 1927 for the development of the Anzac Square project.

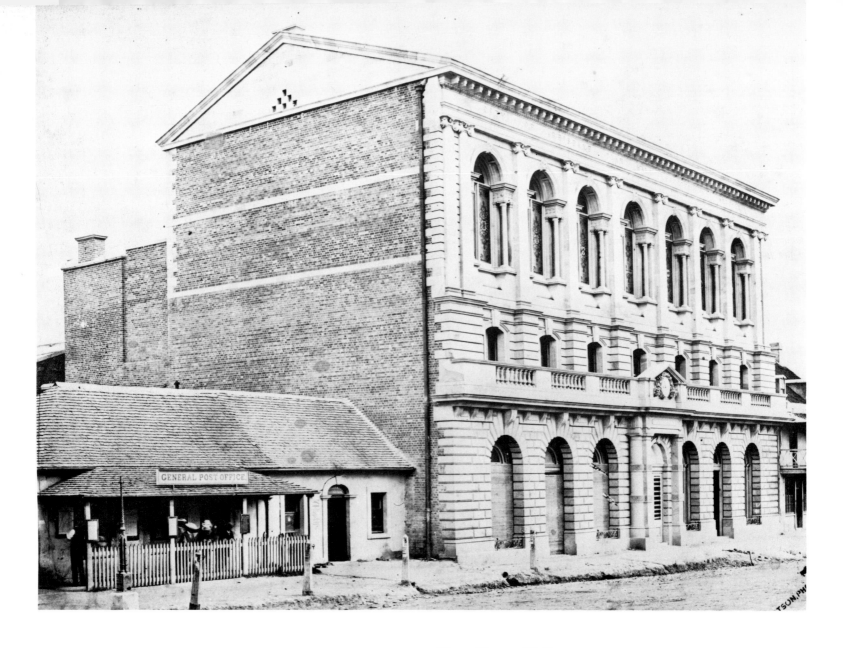

First Town Hall

Prior to Separation, Brisbane residents had become interested in the New South Wales *Municipalities Act* of 1858 and its associated advantages, and they subsequently petitioned the Governor of New South Wales for a system of local government for the town of Brisbane. The proclamation announcing the incorporation of Brisbane appeared in the *New South Wales Government Gazette* of 7 September 1859. The first elections were duly held and the first meeting of the municipal council was held on 13 October 1859 — while Brisbane was still part of New South Wales. John Petrie was unanimously elected the first mayor.

Opposite: *An impressive Victorian symbol of civic pride, the first Town Hall appeared grand among its more humble neighbours such as the adjacent, single storey, convict built structures. Note the decoration on the window glass of the top storey of the Town Hall. This site is now occupied by Lennon's Plaza Hotel. The former Convict Barracks building was located just to the right of the illustration.*

Right: *The Walter Hill Fountain in the Botanic Gardens, c 1910. This illustration is one half of a stereo-scopic view and shows the Victorian style drinking fountain erected in 1867 to provide the first pure drinking water for visitors to the Gardens.*

The council initially was housed in the Police Court building but soon moved to premises in Queen Street near the Victoria Bridge. These were occupied until the new Town Hall was erected in Queen Street just south of the former Convict Barracks building and adjacent to the former solitary cells.

Begun in 1864, this impressive Victorian symbol of civic pride was not completed until 1867. Though it appeared grand among the more humble structures around it, there were serious complaints about its design and construction. Nevertheless, the building survived most of those 'who shook wise heads over its supposed instability and the danger of using it for public gatherings, but it was never useful for any other purpose than Council Chambers and business offices'. The lack of a central hall for public gatherings of all descriptions was keenly felt and eventually the present City Hall, between Adelaide and Ann Streets, was constructed in 1928 to replace it. The old Town Hall was then sold for commercial use and was later demolished. Lennons Plaza Hotel now occupies the site.

Walter Hill Fountain

In 1855 Walter Hill was appointed Director of the Botanical Reserve in Brisbane, which had been set aside in the early years of free settlement on the site of the former penal settlement's Government Garden. Hill was instrumental in increasing the Reserve from its original 25 ha to include river frontage and elevated land to the south-west previously set aside for sale.

Hill experimented with both local and overseas seeds and plants to determine suitability of climate and profitability of cultivation, and one of his most effective plantings was the row of magnificent Bunya pines still bordering the lawn near the main (Edward Street) entrance to the Gardens. These were planted prior to 1861. Hill laid out the Gardens so that the public could gain maximum knowledge and enjoyment from his plantings and in 1867 he erected a Victorian style drinking fountain to provide visitors to the Gardens with the first pure drinking water. Standing about 2 m high, the fountain is constructed of sandstone with marble inlays.

Parliament House

Prior to the first election of the Queensland Parliament in early 1860, an interim Queensland Government was appointed to carry on the machinery of government. The first elected Queensland Parliament met on 22 May 1860 in the former Convict Barracks in Queen Street, which remained the home of Parliament until the present Parliament House in George Street was erected.

The foundation stone of the present magnificent French Renaissance style building was laid on 14 July 1865 and Parliament first met in the new building on 4 August 1868. The design was by Charles Tiffin and was the winning entry in an Australia wide competition for the building with a prize of 200 guineas.

Designed to overlook the nearby gardens and parkland, the main George Street facade was completed first. The frontal colonnade was added in 1880 (for protection from the sun) and the Alice Street wing was added in 1891.

The new Parliament House contained two legislative chambers, one for the Upper House or Legislative Council and one for the Lower House or Legislative Assembly. The nominee Legislative Council was abolished in 1922. A main entrance portico or porte cochere is presently being constructed and the building is undergoing extensive renovations.

The Legislative Council Chamber (Upper House) shortly after completion of Parliament House.

The Reservoir at Roma Street, 1862.

Interior of the Wickham Terrace Service Reservoirs (built 1871 and 1882), which helped augment the inner city water supply service.

A picnic at Enoggera Reservoir.

Brisbane's Early Water Supply

Initially, Brisbane's water supply came from creeks and wells, including the creek which flowed near the localities of the present Roma Street Station and Civic Square to enter the Brisbane River near Creek Street. An earthen dam was constructed across the creek near Tank Street and a pipeline of hollow hardwood logs distributed the water.

With increasing settlement the catchment of the reservoir's water supply soon was built over and in the early 1860s the Municipal Council of Brisbane commissioned the new Enoggera water supply. The first sod of the Enoggera Dam was cut on 18 August 1864 by the Surveyor–General, A.C. Gregory, and the dam was completed in March 1866. Late in August 1866 the 'water was triumphantly turned on to serve the 94 chains of mains reticulating Queen, George, and Edward streets'. And so Brisbane's reticulated water supply began.

The Enoggera Reservoir became a favourite 'drive from Brisbane' and 'the favourite haunt of the sportsman who was lucky enough to come armed with a permit from the Board of Waterworks, which licensed him to use the official boat and destroy the ducks and other wild fowl on the lake; but owing to the rapid decrease in the number of native birds, it has been found necessary to abolish this custom'.

The original section of the Brisbane General Post Office, with the remains of 'gaol hill' visible at the extreme right.

General Post Office

With the growth of Brisbane and surrounding districts, the facilities and accommodation required by the G.P.O. soon outgrew those provided in the convict built quarters near the new Town Hall. In 1871 work began on the present G.P.O. building in Queen Street, on the site of the former Female Factory which was later used as a gaol. The buildings were demolished and 'gaol hill' was levelled prior to the commencement of work on the new building by John Petrie.

The original structure consisted of the northern wing only, opened on 28 September 1872. But rapid expansion of business and the Government's decision to jointly house the two separate Postal and Electric Telegraph departments,

soon required the addition of the matching southern wing, and a central clock tower joined the two. In 1879 the southern wing was opened and housed the newly formed Post and Telegraph Department.

The buildings were constructed of sandstone, local porphyry, and bricks from Petrie's clay pit at Albion, and the upper verandahs featured iron lace balustrading. The G.P.O. building answered well the requirements of the then Postmaster–General, Thomas Lodge Murray-Prior, who said that 'so near the tropics as is Brisbane, it becomes a necessity that a building should be lofty, well ventilated, properly drained and otherwise adapted for the duties to be performed'.

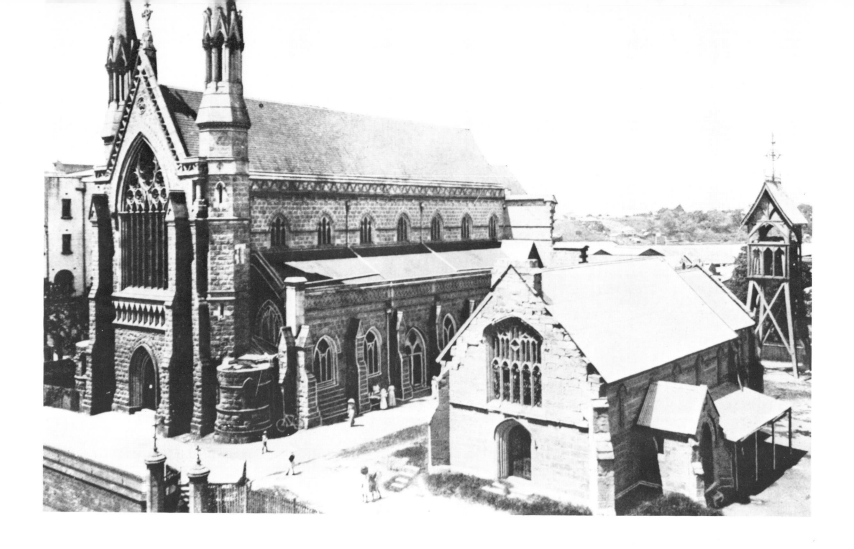

St Stephen's Church and Cathedral

The spiritual well-being of the citizens of early Brisbane was not overlooked and in 1850 St Stephen's Church was completed and dedicated. It was the principal Roman Catholic church in Brisbane until 1874, when the adjacent St Stephen's Cathedral was opened. Old St Stephen's, as it is now known, was built in sandstone to a simple Gothic design attributed to the noted English architect Augustus W. Pugin. The oldest church building extant in Brisbane, it was erected when Brisbane was still part of the Diocese of Sydney.

By 1863 it was found that old St Stephen's was proving inadequate for the requirements of the rapidly increasing Catholic community in Brisbane. It was decided that another church should be built and the foundation stone of the new St Stephen's Cathedral was laid on 26 December 1863, the Feast of St Stephen.

Financial difficulties of the period temporarily hampered progress in 1864–65. In order to raise the much needed funds for the continuance of the construction Dr James Quinn, the first Catholic Bishop of Brisbane, instituted a system of Sunday house-to-house collections which he undertook to subsidise personally pound for pound. Work had progressed far enough by Sunday morning, 17 May 1874, for the new Cathedral to be blessed and opened.

On 5 July 1875 Bishop Quinn blessed old St Stephen's for use as the first Christian Brothers School in Brisbane. In 1880, after increasing attendances at the school, the Brothers moved to Gregory Terrace and established St Joseph's College. Old St Stephen's was subsequently used as a school by the Sisters of Mercy and as a storehouse and church offices. The cathedral is currently being enlarged, and both buildings and grounds are being renovated in conjunction with the adjacent St Stephen's School. The church is now used for smaller ceremonies.

First Permanent Victoria Bridge

Brisbane's first permanent Victoria Bridge, an elaborate lattice girder structure, was opened on 15 June 1874 by the Governor of Queensland, the Marquis of Normanby. The bridge, named in honour of the Queen, linked the north and south sides of the river at the approximate location of the present, third permanent Victoria Bridge. It was fitted with a swinging girder to allow passage of ships with tall masts, but when the tram-lines were laid across the bridge in the 1880s, this girder was fixed in position permanently.

The Victoria Bridge was the project of the relatively new Brisbane Municipal Council, whose enthusiasm for the project appears to have exceeded their wisdom and their purse. Begun in the early 1860s, the project was seriously threatened by a financial crisis in 1866 and the attendant collapse of the Bank of Queensland. In addition, con-struction was hampered by difficulty in locating a firm foundation, and 'more than once during its erection the strong floods which at that time flushed the river undermined the piles'. Though it opened as a toll bridge in 1874, the revenue from the tolls was insufficient to meet the debts and the Queensland Government took it over in 1876. The bridge was returned to the municipality four years later free of debt and of tolls. This first permanent Victoria Bridge collapsed during the height of the 1893 flood.

Opposite: *St Stephen's Church, the oldest church building extant in Brisbane, and St Stephen's Cathedral, begun in 1863 when the smaller structure could no longer accommodate Brisbane's rapidly expanding Catholic community.*

Below: *The first permanent Victoria Bridge opened as a toll bridge in 1874 and the toll station was located to the right of the sign at the entrance to the bridge. The area at the southern end of the bridge is now the site of the new Queensland Cultural Centre.*

This illustration of the new Castlemaine Brewery appeared in **Queensland Punch** *on 1 August 1879.*

Castlemaine Brewery, Milton

In 1878, Messrs Fitzgerald of the Castlemaine Brewery Company in Victoria decided to establish a brewery in Brisbane and formed a partnership with Mr Michael Quinlan of Quinlan Gray and Co. Ltd. Premises for brewing were erected at Milton 'about a mile from the city, on the Southern and Western Railway', on the site still occupied by the Brewery in Milton Road.

In 1916 the company confined its operations entirely to brewing and to wines and spirits. In 1928 the Castlemaine Brewery and Quinlan, Gray and Co. Ltd merged with another early Queensland brewer Perkins and Co. Ltd, and on 1 August 1928 Castlemaine Perkins Ltd began business operations. This merging of two of the oldest businesses in Queensland at the time was a significant event in the State's commercial history.

Patrick Perkins, who had established breweries in both Toowoomba and Brisbane prior to the erection of the Castlemaine Brewery at Milton, entered Parliament in 1874 as the Member for Aubigny in the Legislative Assembly. He may have had an advantage over any political opponent, as it was reported how a railway contractor named Garett 'had a large work on hand at the period of a general election, and being an intimate associate of Perkins what could be more simple than to load up half a dozen trucks with Perkins' XXX ale and a vast number of navvies and tour Aubigny electorate . . . In the opinion of the navvies it was good beer and the owner worthy of an unlimited number of votes. Perkins won that election hands down'. 'Castlemaine XXXX', now brewed by Bond Corporation Holdings Limited, continues to be a firm favourite with Queenslanders.

Ormiston House

Louis Hope, a former captain in the Coldstream Guards and seventh son of the Earl of Hopetoun, emigrated to New South Wales in 1843 and five years later moved to Moreton Bay, where he acquired land at Ormiston in 1853–54.

An early slab hut erected on the property subsequently became the kitchen of the fine colonial house that Hope erected. Skilled craftsmen are said to have been brought from Scotland to build the seventeen room house, constructed of hand-made bricks on a stone foundation and with wide surrounding verandahs supported by paired

Ormiston House prior to restoration.

turned columns of cedar. A timber chapel, an overseer's cottage and a gatekeeper's cottage in brick were also built on the property. To develop Ormiston's magnificent surrounding gardens, Hope used many rare and beautiful imported plants.

In 1862–63 Hope planted twenty acres of sugar cane at Ormiston and built his own sugar mill. The first successful commercial production of sugar in Australia was obtained by Hope in 1864. Using Kanakas to work in the fields, Hope continued his enterprise with mixed success, learning mainly by trial and error and spending thousands of pounds in the process. Following a dispute over the crushing of another's cane, Hope dismantled his mill and subsequently returned to England. Ormiston was not sold, however, until some years after Hope's death in 1894. Eventually, in 1959, Ormiston was bought by the Discalced Carmelite Nuns who erected a monastery in the 27 acre grounds. Ormiston House is now maintained by the Ormiston House Restoration Association, which opens the home to the public.

Bark and Slab Huts

Many early settlers with no previous experience of bush life had to erect their own living quarters when they settled on the land. Readily available materials were generally used for construction, and in a timbered locality the quickest and simplest house to erect was a bark hut. 'Hints to new Settlers' were included in the *Queensland Agricultural Journal* in 1913, based on the previous 'personal, practical experience' of the writer. Instructions were provided on selecting the right trees, how to fell trees, take off a sheet of bark, split slabs, rails and shingles, and build your hut — bark or slab.

The bark hut could be built in a day. Nails were seldom used 'as the heads draw through the bark unless backed with a square of leather, for which old boots come in handy'. The bark hut was often 'floored with white-ant bed made into a sort of mortar with an admixture of cow dung. This makes a durable floor'.

From his own experiences and that of other numerous pioneers, the writer in the *Queensland Agricultural Journal* further advised that 'the bark hut is certainly a very comfortable rest-house for a couple of young bachelors, but a time arrives when other people have to be considered — mothers, sisters, wives. For the comfort of a man's family, some better habitation must be provided, and the first step in this direction is the erection of a slab and shingle house. Such a house can be cheaply built out of local timber, and may be made as comfortable as the future building, which will be of sawn timber, galvanised iron roofing, etc.'.

In slab huts, the floor could be 'left in a state of nature', laid with dressed slabs, or laid with a cement of white-ant hill or of the ant bed mixed with cow dung. 'When this is well puddled with water, and laid on smoothly to a thickness of 4 to 6 in., it soon hardens and makes a capital floor'.

Spring Hill

The earliest spread of settlement occurred in those areas closest to or within easy access to the centre of Brisbane, such as Kangaroo Point, South Brisbane, Spring Hill and Petrie Terrace.

The first land sales for the Spring Hill area were held in 1856. Allotments available included high land overlooking the centre of the town and with views to the distant hills, and it was on these ridges that fine residences of the day were built. But in the lower areas modest 'workers' dwellings' developed, constructed of timber, elevated on stumps following the hilly terrain and with steeply pitched roofs. Many were on very small allotments. The main building activity occurred between about 1856 and 1900 and by this time Spring Hill had become one of the most densely populated areas of Brisbane.

A change in use of many of the finer buildings gradually occurred with their conversion to boarding houses, schools, specialist medical centres and hospitals. With further expansion of the city, office and other commercial accommodation has encroached and many of the old buildings are fast disappearing. The Brisbane City Council, however, is presently investigating ways in which the character of the area will not be completely destroyed during re-development.

Opposite: *Bark and slab huts on Cleveland Road in the early 1870s. These 'humpies' were easily constructed in a day without nails and with floors made from a mortar of white ant bed and cow dung.*

Below: *Spring Hill viewed across Petrie Bight. Queen Street is at the left, Ann Street is behind the two storey hotel at the centre of the picture, and Boundary Street is prominent towards the right. The larger, two storey structures stand on the ridges whilst the smaller, single storey dwellings are located in the lower areas.*

Above: *A view of the Petrie Terrace area from Enoggera Road, c 1873–75. Petrie Terrace is at the top left, Hale and Caxton Streets intersect towards the left of the picture, and Milton Road is visible between the cemetery and the river. Part of the cemetery site is now occupied by the Lang Park football grounds, but the school on the corner of Hale Street and Milton Road is still in use and many of the dwellings survive.*

Opposite: *A view in 1880 of the first houses built at Indooroopilly, where the Southern and Western Railway connecting Brisbane with Ipswich and the Darling Downs crossed the Brisbane River via the Albert Railway Bridge.*

Petrie Terrace

The main development of Petrie Terrace occurred between about 1860 and 1900 with the erection of modest 'working-class' homes. Most of these were small timber homes on small allotments and many were built on the street line. Streets were also very narrow — it is believed that the original large suburban allotments were re-subdivided into the maximum number of building sites with the resultant small allotments, narrow streets and tiny service lanes. A few terrace houses were erected in the area, as were shops, a school, a hotel and churches.

The area developed on the western slope of the ridge running from today's Milton Road to Musgrave Road at the Normanby Junction. On the eastern slope was the Gaol and Victoria Barracks and to the west of the area across Hale Street was the Paddington Cemetery. This was relocated in 1916 and the present Lang Park football grounds occupy part of this former cemetery site.

Suburban Expansion

As Brisbane developed and grew, the population spread further outwards and eventually larger holdings were broken up into small suburban allotments. Ronald Lawson in *Brisbane in the 1890s* states that 'between 1886 and 1891 the population of the old municipality of Brisbane decreased by over 2,000, as many moved to homes further from the centre. The majority of the people, however, still lived reasonably close . . . in 1891, 92.2 per cent of the population living within a 10-mile radius of the city centre in fact lived within five miles . . .

'The availability of public transport partly moulded the direction of suburban expansion and conversely, closer settlement was often followed by the provision of transport services. The existence of trunk railway lines, such as the Ipswich line through the south-western suburbs, preceded residential expansion . . . In 1892 there were 30 daily services from Indooroopilly to the city.'

Queensland's first railway, between Ipswich and present-day Grandchester, 21 miles to the west, was opened on 31 July 1865. In 1867 the line reached Toowoomba on the Darling Downs, but it was not until 1875 that the line was extended to Brisbane. The opening of the railway was the impetus for the subsequent development of suburban Indooroopilly.

'The first train carrying passengers from Brisbane started at 6.30 a.m. on 14th June, 1875. The line was not quite finished [and] everything was makeshift . . . The bridge over the Brisbane River at Indooroopilly was unfinished, and passengers, goods, etc., were conveyed across the river in a punt'. The station at Indooroopilly was some distance from the punt which was located at the bottom of a 'very steep pinch'. The *Brisbane Courier* reported that 'the punt . . . cannot be considered altogether a desirable conveyance, as the bulk of the space is occupied by a couple of drays conveying luggage, each drawn by two powerful horses, upon the complete docility of which the safety of the transit depends'. The Albert Railway Bridge subsequently superceded the punt.

A recent view of the ruins of the penal settlement established in the 1860s on St Helena Island in Moreton Bay.

St Helena

Towards the end of 1865 it was decided that a new quarantine station on St Helena Island in Moreton Bay should replace the station at Dunwich. At this time, to relieve the overcrowding in Brisbane's gaol, some prisoners were confined on the prison hulk *Proserpine* anchored near the mouth of the Brisbane River. It was these prisoners who provided the labour for the construction of the new establishment, begun in February 1866.

The Government decided at the end of 1866 that St Helena would become a penal establishment instead and on 14 May 1867 it was proclaimed a place 'whereat offenders under order of sentence of hard labour or penal servitude might be detained'. The first prisoners were confined there 6 days later. St Helena was to be the place where long sentence prisoners from Brisbane Gaol were sent, but the first such men did not arrive until the end of 1869.

St Helena eventually became the principal prison in Queensland, accommodating over 300 prisoners, and for many years different trades were carried out in workshops there. The island comprised about 202 ha and a considerable amount of this area was under cultivation, one of the main crops being sugar cane. The island had its own crushing mill, but after some time the cultivation of cane was discontinued — some have said it was because it was a favourite hiding place for troublesome prisoners.

In 1921 the workshops and most prisoners were transferred to Brisbane Gaol in Boggo Road Dutton Park, but a few prisoners were kept at St Helena which was converted to a prison farm. This survived until 1933 when all the prisoners were transferred to Boggo Road Gaol. The penal settlement structures subsequently fell into ruins. In October 1979 the island was declared a national park — the first in Queensland to protect a major historical site — and is now open to the public.

Boggo Road Gaol

The old gaol at Petrie Terrace, first occupied on 5 November 1860, became increasingly overcrowded until the inmates were transferred to a new gaol at Dutton Park, then on the southern outskirts of Brisbane, on 2 July 1883. Begun in 1881, the buildings were of locally made brick with concrete foundations, and stone from the demolished Petrie Terrace gaol buildings was also used. Boundary walls of brick were about 6 m high. The original complex consisted of 57 cells, gaolers' and warders' quarters, hospital, workshop, kitchens, store, debtors' and warders' room and underground tank. The prisoners held in the old Brisbane Gaol at the time of construction of this Boggo Road complex were those awaiting trial, debtors, criminal lunatics, and prisoners required as cooks to keep the establishment clean and in order. All other prisoners 'eligible for transfer' to the new gaol were temporarily accommodated at St Helena. Boggo Road Gaol is now the State's main prison.

An early view of the interior of Boggo Road Gaol at Dutton Park, opened in 1883 and now Queensland's main prison.

The Joss House at Breakfast Creek, shortly after it opened in 1884.

Joss House, Breakfast Creek

Small numbers of Chinese first arrived in Queensland in the 1840s but in the 1870s they began arriving in significantly large numbers, mainly to take advantage of the gold rushes. The Europeans were not favourably disposed towards the Chinese, who were both physically and culturally different, and the majority of whom were intent on making their money and returning with it as quickly as possible to China. The Chinese thus tended to maintain their own way of life in Queensland, continuing their own customs rather than adopting new ones, and functioning 'as a united and independent social entity'. The Chinese community itself was fragmented further into its own groups and secret societies, based on such things as place of origin, lineage and wealth. Most of the Chinese emigrants were brought to Queensland under a bondage system, in debt to Chinese capitalists at home or in Australia for their passage.

The Temple of the Holy Triad at Breakfast Creek is one of the few remaining Joss Houses in Queensland built by these early Chinese. Opened in 1884, it closed in 1930 but was reopened by the Chinese community of Brisbane in 1966 after extensive renovations. Special furnishings, ornaments and a full time caretaker were brought from Hong Kong. Firecrackers and noise makers 'scared the devil and his evil spirits out of the Joss House and allowed the return of the gods of Wealth and Medicine and Knowledge'. Monday 13 June at 2.00 am was chosen as the re-opening time 'after consultation with the Chinese almanac, the three gods and the elders of the Joss House in Sydney'. The building is now open to the public for inspection.

An early view of the fountain at the junction of Eagle, Queen and Wharf Streets, erected as a memorial to a fireman who died from burns received during a Queen Street fire in 1877.

Eagle Street Fountain

On 23 March 1877, Brisbane's Volunteer Fire Brigade attended a fire in a grocery store in Queen Street. But it was a Friday night, and the water from the Enoggera Reservoir was turned off, rendering the Brigade's apparatus useless. Firemen, police and employees of the burning store worked to prevent the fire from spreading to nearby properties, but during this work a cask of rum exploded and one of the most energetic firemen, James Mooney, received severe burns from which he died the following day.

Public sympathy ran high and collections were begun for funds for a monument to Mooney. In June 1878 the Municipal Council Improvement Committee was instructed to deal with a proposed fountain at the intersection of Eagle and Queen Streets in Mooney's memory. Both the Council and the citizens were to provide the funds for the project.

However, when the fountain was completed in April 1880 it bore a tablet stating that it was erected by the Corporation and carried the names of the Mayor and Aldermen, but no reference to Mooney. A hostile citizen wrote to the editor of the *Brisbane Courier* on 17 May 1880 about this situation, stating that he 'would like to see a balance sheet showing the amount of subscriptions received outside of the Corporation as well as the amount subscribed by it. I think such a statement would show that the tablet is too much like many a tombstone i.e., that what it states is not exactly truth'.

This delightful example of a Victorian drinking fountain is still referred to as the Mooney Memorial Fountain. The Mooney Memorial, however, is in Toowong Cemetery.

Queen Street and the Boom

During the 'boom period' of the 1880s many fine buildings sprang up in Brisbane and considerably changed the character of its central business area. Fine warehouses and commercial premises were erected, new hotels appeared and old ones were enlarged and improved. Even by 1884 Theophilus Pugh in his *Almanac* remarked that 'not only in its architectural aspect is the city improved; its pavements are now alive with pedestrians, whilst so numerous have become the vehicles that the streets are much too narrow to hold them; a feeling being naturally aroused that the first layers of the city were as narrow minded as the thoroughfares they laid down . . . Additional traffic facilities will shortly be afforded by the tramways, to be laid from Woolloongabba along Stanley Street, South Brisbane, the Victoria Bridge, Queen Street and the Valley to the Waterloo Hotel. The demand for city and suburban land has continued unabated . . .'.

The following year Pugh reported that 'never in the history of Brisbane have building operations been more

Queen Street c 1890, showing the then Town Hall (right) and adjacent buildings, including the premises of the Colonial Mutual Life Assurance Society on its left (a menswear store in 1988).

A view of Queen Street across the intersection with Albert Street c 1899, showing buildings erected in the 1880s between the Town Hall and Albert Street, on the site of the former Convict Barracks building.

active than at present, nor have structures of such proportions been thought of. Buildings are arising in all directions worthy of any town in the world . . . Queen Street has been further improved by some fine premises adjoining the Town Hall, and in the same street there are some fine vacant sites which will probably shortly be built on. In the suburbs building continues at a great rate, and the Sandgate line may be said to pass through a town almost to its terminus at the sea side'.

In 1883 a fine building was erected for the Colonial Mutual Life Assurance Society, adjacent to the Town Hall, on the site of Brisbane's first G.P.O. and the former solitary cells of the penal settlement. The building was designed by architect Richard Gailey and still survives today.

The new buildings erected in the early 1880s between the Town Hall and Albert Street, on the site of the former Convict Barracks, were described in 1887 as 'a pile of buildings that would do credit to any city in Australasia', and were occupied by the shops of drapers, booksellers and photographers. Many of these buildings still exist.

The Mansions

In 1889 a fine row of six terrace houses was erected in George Street near Parliament House, the Botanic Gardens, the exclusive Queensland Club and the new Bellevue Hotel (recently demolished). This was one of the city's most attractive localities. It is thought that The Mansions was erected for three members of Parliament at the time, and each residence was to include three reception rooms and at least ten other rooms, excluding servants' quarters. The earliest occupants included Queensland's pioneer woman doctor, Lilian Cooper, other surgeons and physicians, dentists, a day school and a boarding house.

The Mansions is constructed of red brick with decoration in Oamaru (New Zealand) limestone, including ornamental cats on the parapet overlooking the city. The building's corner position is impressive, with arcaded balconies stretching along both facades at two levels, and an arched

The Mansions, erected as six terrace houses in 1889, was designed to suit the local climate. The architect, G.H.M. Addison, also designed the Exhibition Building and Concert Hall (q.v.) and Cumbooquepa (q.v.).

parapet above. The building is topped by paired roof dormers echoing the arcades and alternating with paired entries at ground level. The design, giving deep shading without obstructing ventilation, is well suited to the local climate.

By the time of the Second World War, the terraces provided mainly boarding house accommodation. After the war, the State Government acquired the building and converted The Mansions for use as offices. More recently, the rear attached sections were demolished, the Mansions refurbished, and the space leased out for a variety of uses including a restaurant, a bookshop, a women's club and a National Trust gift shop.

The former Queensland National Bank c. 1890, one of the finest examples of Renaissance architecture in Australia.

Queensland National Bank

The Queensland National Bank (1872–1947) constructed its magnificent head office building at the corner of Queen and Creek streets in 1881–85. The 'Q.N.' was the first trading bank to have its Board of Directors and its head office in Brisbane, and it very quickly dominated Queensland finances in a way unequalled by any other Australian bank.

The Q.N. was closely associated with the Queensland Government. Awarded the Queensland Government account in 1879 it subsequently both supported and was supported by the Government, carrying out its banking business for forty-two years. When Thomas McIlwraith became Premier in 1879 he resigned his position on the bank's Board and his place was taken by his brother-in-law Sir Arthur Palmer. In the early 1880s the bank's Board contained two members of McIlwraith's Cabinet, and the Chairman of Directors was a member of the Legislative Council.

Difficult financial conditions in Australia and Britain resulted in the bank's suspension of payment on 15 May 1893. The bank reopened 79 days later, but another reconstruction was necessary in 1897, with Government support, and eventually the bank's finances and good name were restored. The Queensland National Bank united with the National Bank of Australasia on 1 January 1948 and the former Q.N. headquarters then became the Brisbane Office of the National Bank of Australasia.

The building is of local sandstone, with columns and carved work of Oamaru limestone. The internal chamber receives natural light through a leaded glass dome and is approached by a corridor with a coffered ceiling vault. The building is regarded as one of the finest examples of Italian Renaissance architecture in Australia.

School of Arts

In 1872, the Queensland National Bank purchased the site at the Corner of Queen and Creek Streets from the School of Arts and Mechanics Institute, which in turn, in 1873, bought the Servants Home in Ann Street, dating from the 1860s. The building was improved in 1877, when the double height verandahs were added, and the School of Arts opened in its new premises in 1878. At the time, there were 600–700 subscribers and a library of 'some 7000 volumes'.

The object of the School of Arts was 'the advancement of culture and the best form of entertainment'. As well as its lending library, the School of Arts offered lectures on a wide variety of topics, exhibitions (both science and arts and crafts), a literary circle and drawing classes. By 1884, additions were made to accommodate a Technical College established in association with the School of Arts, catering for hundreds of students in a wide range of subjects, including cooking, languages and mathematics. By 1902, the Technical College had progressed to the extent that it was transferred from the jurisdiction of the School of Arts to the State education system.

In 1937, shops were added to the front of the building and, later, offices were built above these. For many years the beauty of the old building was hidden, but in 1983 the Brisbane City Council, who had acquired the building and library in 1965 and had operated the Council's Central City Library from here, began the slow process of restoration. The City Council Library was relocated to the City Hall, and the old School of Arts building now houses the Queensland Conservation Council and the Craft Council of Queensland.

Above: *The former Servants Home, dating from the 1860s, was added to and 'improved' in 1877 and reopened as the School of Arts in 1878. The building has recently been restored by the present owner, the Brisbane City Council.*

A.U.S.N. Company Building

Brisbane's dependency on shipping meant dependency on shipping companies and in the early years this meant southern companies such as the Australasian Steam Navigation Company. In 1881 the Queensland Steamship Company was formed by several companies which were operating in Queensland by this time, and six years later this company amalgamated with the A.S.N. Company and overseas interests to form the Australasian United Steam Navigation Company.

In 1889 an imposing building was erected in Brisbane for the newly formed company, designed by the architects A.L. and G. McCreedy of Sydney in Victorian Classic Revival style. A fine cupola surmounted the north-eastern tower, and verandahs on two levels were concessions to the local climate. The building was located close to the company's wharf and the levels reached by Brisbane's major floods are recorded on the tower. The accompanying photograph was taken during the 1893 flood. The building was subsequently occupied by Macdonald Hamilton and Company, managing agents for the A.U.S.N. Company from 1915. Recently known as Naldham House, it is presently part of a redevelopment project.

Customs House

The active development of the Port of Brisbane began with free settlement and in 1846 a branch of the Customs Department was established at Moreton Bay. On 24 February 1849 the present site was chosen for the erection of a new Customs House and the one storey building was opened on 26 March 1850. But the rapidly expanding Port of Brisbane soon outgrew this small building.

Work on a new Customs House on the same site began in 1886, but the building, constructed by J. Petrie and Son, was not completed until 1889. This grand new building 'combined convenience facilities together with a beautiful appearance both from Queen Street and the River', and despite some unsympathetic modernisation 'retains the distinction externally and internally of being ranked among the most ornate and prettily situated Customs Houses of the world'. The building is a fine example of Classic Revival architecture and perhaps its most striking feature is the well proportioned copper dome.

The former Australasian United Steam Navigation Company's building was erected close to the Company's wharf near Petrie Bight. The heights reached by the Brisbane River during the city's major floods are recorded on the tower. This photo was taken during the 1893 Flood.

The Treasury Building was erected in three stages from 1885 to 1928. The William Street section, viewed here from the northern entrance to the Victoria Bridge, was completed first.

A fine example of Classic Revival architecture, the Customs House is crowned by a magnificent copper dome and was completed in 1889.

Treasury Building

Work began in 1885 on excavation of the site of the former convict built Guard Houses, Officers' Quarters and Military Barracks, for the construction of the new Treasury Building. The building was erected in three stages from 1885 to 1928. The William Street section was erected first and was occupied in 1889; the remaining Elizabeth Street frontage was erected in 1890–93; and the remaining George and Queen Street facades were erected in 1922–28.

The *Queenslander* on 12 October 1889 reported that 'before entering upon erection of the Treasury Buildings the Government, anxious to get as perfect a design as possible, threw the work open to competition and offered prizes for the three best designs. A large number of architects residing in different colonies forwarded drawings to Brisbane, and out of them three were finally approved . . . Mr J.J. Clark, Colonial Architect, was appointed to prepare plans embodying the best features of the three successful designs. The result of his labours, modified and altered perhaps considerably, was the plan from which the Treasury Buildings were erected'.

Designed in Italian Renaissance style, the sandstone building has its accommodation set deeply behind arches and colonnades which protect from the sun and rain but do not obstruct cooling ventilation. The Treasury is one of the finest buildings in Australia and occupies an entire city block.

After 1886, immigrants arriving in Brisbane (Opposite) were accommodated at Yungabah, Kangaroo Point (Above).

Yungabah

Yungabah was built by the Queensland Government in 1885–86 as accommodation for immigrants and is still used for this purpose. When constructed, the two storey brick building with decorative cast iron balustrading provided 'two wards for married couples on each side of a central hall on the ground floor, one ward for single men and one for single women on the first floor; each ward is provided with separate day-room, kitchen, store, lavatory and bath accommodation and exercise yard. In the centre of the building are the administrative offices, with cellars for luggage, and at the ends are the warders' houses. The whole provides accommodation for about 500 immigrants'.

The hostel was built on the promontory at Kangaroo Point, an ideal location for its purpose. However the Story Bridge was later constructed close to Yungabah, which is now situated below the bridge. It is said that some of the workmen were accommodated here during the construction of the bridge and that Yungabah was used as a hospital for the defence forces in both world wars.

Arrival of Immigrants, 1888

The arrival of immigrants in Brisbane and their reaction to their new, strange surroundings, was described by an observer in 1888.

'Very lovely and attractive must the land appear to the immigrant arriving at this season [May–September] after six weeks of the weary monotony of the ocean steamer or twice as long a spell of it in a sailing vessel, and now looking upon his future home, the land of promise smiling and bright in the glittering air.

'The landing of immigrants is a scene of great interest, and suggestive of many reflections upon the contrast between the surroundings and conditions of their past and of their future homes, and upon their prospects in the New World, where a measure of success is attainable by all. The new arrivals are transhipped in the river from the big steamer to a tug, and from that are landed at the Government depôt. When leaving the steamer, and as they step ashore, they are passed to the depôt by the officials, and there are lodged until they find work or friends, or are forwarded to other depôts

up-country. As they come ashore they are in striking contrast to the native Australians and adopted colonials present, and for a considerable time the character of "new chum" is as plainly evidenced by their appearance and dress as if they were labelled with the title. Whole families, groups of young men and women, and the inevitable lonely ones file down the gangways — some searching for friendly faces in those around them, others looking about in simple curiosity, all interested and observant. No sooner is the luggage landed, and a few formalities gone through with the officials, than they are out into the town, "looking round" — the first stage in the process of merging themselves in the New World community'.

Fort Lytton was developed as an intricate defence complex near the mouth of the Brisbane River, but with the introduction of sophisticated modern defence techniques the fort became obsolete.

Fort Lytton

Queensland's small population and isolation made her sensitive during the 1870s to European expansion in the Pacific and to persistent fears of war with Russia. The main concern was with the occupation of New Guinea and Torres Straits, especially when her greatest security lay in 'the difficulty of approach to any place of sufficient importance to invite attack'.

In 1877 a report on Queensland's defence recommended that Brisbane should be protected by defences at the mouth of the river. Fort Lytton was subsequently developed and became a main line of defence until after the First World War and a second line of defence during the Second World War. Fort Lytton was an intricate defence complex surrounded by a moat which connected with the Brisbane River.

With the development of sophisticated modern defence equipment and techniques, Fort Lytton became obsolete in Australia's defence network. The site eventually was disposed of by the Commonwealth and is now part of the Ampol Petroleum Company's Oil Refinery. Aware of the Fort's heritage value, the Company has made the complex available for public inspection.

The Queensland Navy

After much debate, the Queensland Parliament in November 1882 voted £60 000 for the purchase of two gunboats which were subsequently built at Newcastle on Tyne and were called the *Gayundah* and *Paluma* (Aboriginal for 'lightning' and 'thunder'). They were twin screw vessels with a designed maximum speed of 10 knots and each had a displacement of 365.8 tonnes and was 36.5 m long, 7.9 m beam and 2.8 m deep. Ready first, *Gayundah* sailed from Newcastle on Tyne in November 1884 and arrived in Brisbane on 27 March 1885. She was the first ship of any Australian colony afforded the privilege of wearing the White Ensign and Penant of Her Majesty's Fleet.

A volunteer Queensland Naval Brigade had been formed at home whilst *Gayundah* was on passage and in 1886–87 Naval Brigade Stores were built at Kangaroo Point. These two two-storey buildings, clad with corrugated iron over a timber framework, rested on foundation walls of stone with concrete footings. The site was the base of the Queensland Marine Defence Force until the formation of the Royal Australian Navy, and comprised a gun battery for training, ship repair and torpedo workshops, boatslip and wharf. During the Second World War the Depot was used by the Royal Australian Navy to store and maintain torpedoes for use in the Pacific.

The Naval Depot was located at the base of the cliffs at Kangaroo Point below St Mary's Church, and the crews of the two gunboats attended the church via steps up the cliff. A simple, Early English Gothic Revival style church constructed of porphyry stone, it opened in 1873, was damaged during a cyclone in 1892, was repaired and enlarged, and rededicated in 1893.

*A view of the Botanic Gardens towards Kangaroo Point, c 1892, with the S.S. **Natone** in the foreground. The Queensland gunboat **Gayundah** lies at anchor in the river, in front of the Naval Brigade Stores at the foot of the Kangaroo Point cliffs. The steps leading up the cliff face to St Mary's Church above, which is undergoing repair, are still in use. Fire damaged one of the Naval Depot buildings in late 1987.*

Petrie Bight and part of the City Reach of the Brisbane River in the 1880s.

Brisbane by Steamer in the 1880s

'In the visitor reaching Brisbane by steamer, the first object that excites attention and elicits admiration is the noble stream on which the city stands and after which it is named. From the mouth of the river, at the township of Lytton, the distance to the wharves is about fifteen miles . . . Rounding the last corner, we see to the right some imposing residences; on the left is the Kangaroo Point Slip, and further on, facing the stone quarries that nestle beneath the heights of Bowen Terrace, the new Immigration Depot Reserve. With some difficulty and at a very slow pace, the vessel swings round Kangaroo Point Corner and the main portion of the city is before us. The British India Steam Navigation Company which is subsidised by the Queensland Government to carry mails *via* Torres Straits, has lately built the only wharf on the Kangaroo Point side. With the exception of the narrow tongue of land that constitutes the ''Point'' proper, this bank is too steep to be favourable for wharf construction, and the

The South Brisbane Reach of the river, with the coal wharves in the foreground and the adjacent Dry Dock in the distance.

river frontage is chiefly occupied by private residences . . .

'On the opposite side are the wharves of Howard, Smith and Co., of Gibbs, Bright and Co., of the Queensland Shipping Company, and the two Australian Steam Navigation wharves, in the order named. Further on is the Inspector of Harbours and Rivers, with a small wharf attached; and the Botanical Gardens end the reach. In the next one is the Government House Domain on the north side . . .

'On the opposite or South Brisbane bank a fine wharf has been erected for the Corporation near the Dry Dock; hard by is the terminus of the South Brisbane Railway, which brings coal down to the vessels from the neighbourhood of Ipswich . . . The chief trades of the city are represented by iron foundries, shipbuilding yards, saw-mills, masonry and rope works; iceworks also are naturally numerous. The wood and coal consumed in the city come chiefly by rail from the neighbourhood of Oxley and of Ipswich . . .'.

South Brisbane Dry Dock

A Dry Dock, designed to service both sailing vessels and steam vessels, was built at South Brisbane in 1878–81. It was constructed of sandstone, granite, cement, hardwood blocks and puddled clay, and was built by H. Overend on behalf of the Queensland Government. Extensions provided for in the original plans were carried out during the 1880s.

Early ship repair work in Brisbane was carried out by several small slips at places such as Lytton, Queensport and Kangaroo Point. The Government's enterprising decision to build the South Brisbane Dry Dock reflected the optimism prevalent in the young colony at this time and answered a prime need in the progressive, thriving seaport of Brisbane.

With progress in world technology and the consequential increase in the length and tonnage of ships, as well as other changes, the use of the South Brisbane Dock eventually became limited. It remained Brisbane's main dry dock until the opening of the Cairncross Dock in the 1940s, and it now forms part of the Queensland Maritime Museum complex. The dock is still in its original condition and its caisson is still in working condition. The Museum is open for public inspection.

Ships in the South Brisbane Dry Dock, viewed from Stanley Street. The Dock is now part of the Queensland Maritime Museum, adjacent to the World Expo 88 site.

Brisbane Grammar Schools

The *Grammar Schools Act of* 1860 provided that any municipality in Queensland wherein £1000 was privately subscribed for the establishment of a grammar school was entitled to claim a grant of £2000 from the Government plus an annual endowment of £500. The first grammar school in Queensland was established at Ipswich in 1864 and in the same year a subscription list was begun in Brisbane.

The foundation stone of the first Brisbane Grammar School (in Roma Street) was laid on 29 February 1868 and the school opened on 1 February 1869. However, when the railway was subsequently constructed from Ipswich to Brisbane, the Roma Street Railway Station complex soon encroached upon the school. In 1880 the foundation stone of the present school in Gregory Terrace was laid by the then Chairman of Trustees, Sir Charles Lilley.

The new school building, a handsome brick structure with sandstone dressings and a slate roof, was designed by the architect James Cowlishaw in Victorian Gothic Revival style. A stone porch led into the Great Hall with its hammar beam roof and excellent 'High Victorian' stained glass windows containing 'pictures of the Queen [Victoria] and prominent English worthies'. A separate library building, designed in a romantic Elongated Gothic style and harmonising with the earlier buildings, was erected as a War Memorial in 1923.

In 1881 Prince Edward (later Duke of Clarence and Avondale) and Prince George (later King George V) visited the school and planted two trees which still survive along the main drive.

Adjacent in Gregory Terrace is Brisbane Girls Grammar School. The foundation stone was laid on 28 February 1883, the day of the annual commemoration of the foundation of the Brisbane Grammar School. The Brisbane Girls Grammer School (below) was designed by the architect Richard Gailey.

Stromness

Hugh L. Moar was an early Brisbane ferryman and ship-wright who, by the early 1880s, had established his own Patent Slip at Cross Street, Kangaroo Point. The Moar's home was located nearby in Cairns Street, Kangaroo Point, and was built probably in the 1870s. A modest Victorian timber residence, its rooms and corridors were simple and small, and the steps to the attic narrow and steep, probably reflecting the influence of the boatbuilder. Abundant lattice work screening to surrounding verandahs and sub-floor area provided shade, privacy and protection from the weather whilst still allowing circulation of cooling air.

When the demolition of Stromness was imminent it was relocated to Early Street Historical Village at Norman Park, where it is now open for public inspection.

Both Stromness (Right) and Auchenflower House (Below) have been relocated from their original sites to Early Street Historical Village at Norman Park. The photo of Stromness is one half of a stereoscopic view entitled 'In Mrs Moar's garden, Kangaroo Point, 1914'. The illustration of Auchenflower House appeared in the **Queenslander** *on 8 August 1891.*

Auchenflower House

One of the most controversial figures in Queensland's history — pastoralist, politician and entrepreneur Sir Thomas McIlwraith — resided at Auchenflower House during some of the turbulent years of his career. A good example of a Victorian colonial gentleman's residence, it was surrounded by attractively decorated verandahs and included a ball room, billiard room, smoking rooms and piazza. The fine home and its several outbuildings such as coach house, stables and porter's lodge, were set in large grounds only a few miles from the centre of Brisbane. The surrounding suburb which developed later took its name from this grand old home.

From the mid-1930s the residence was occupied as a Carmelite monastery until the Order moved to Ormiston in the 1960s. Once again Mr Stanley Hancock saved part of Queensland's heritage from demolition when he relocated part of Auchenflower House to Early Street Historical Village at Norman Park. The interior of this section is unusual and ornate with varnished timber walls, ceilings, fretwork and trusses, and the room space continuing up to the crown of the roof. The building is open for public inspection and is available for functions.

Miegunyah

Miegunyah was built about 1884–85 as the home of Herbert and George Perry, partners in the firm of Perry Brothers, ironmongers and merchants. It was built at Bowen Hills, then known as Breakfast Creek, on land owned by their father, William, a retired ironmonger and later a member of the Legislative Council, who lived nearby. Miegunyah remained in the Perry family until it was sold in 1926 after the death of Herbert.

The single storey timber residence is surrounded by verandahs with lavish cast iron decoration and it sits on brick piers, with honeycomb infil screening the sub-floor area whilst still allowing its ventilation. This charming old house was threatened with demolition for redevelopment of the site in 1960. A courageous band of ladies, the Queensland Women's Historical Association, campaigned for its preservation and by 1967 had raised sufficient funds to save it. The Association has since restored the building and furnished it 'in the gracious style of the Victorian era' — a memorial to the pioneer women of Queensland. The home is now open as a 'Folk Museum' for public viewing.

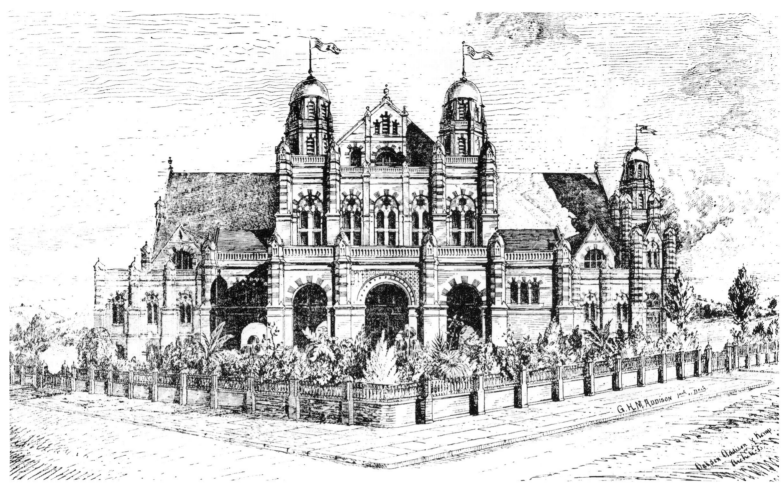

*This illustration of the proposed Exhibition Building and Concert Hall appeared in the **Queenslander** on 4 April 1891.*

Exhibition Building and Concert Hall (Later Queensland Museum)

In 1888 fire destroyed the premises of the Queensland National Association at Bowen Hills and an ambitious programme for the erection of a new Exhibition Building was subsequently embarked upon. Architect for the project was G.H.M. Addison of the 'established Melbourne firm' of Oakden, Addison and Kemp. The contract for construction by John Quinn was signed on 9 February 1891 and '23 weeks only expired from then until what may be called completion . . . in building circles the feat is regarded as highly meritorious, and one which furnished a building record for Queensland if not Australia'.

The new building included both an Exhibition Hall and a Concert Hall and was designed in a flamboyant Victorian Revival style. The *Brisbane Courier* on 15 August 1891 reported that 'the ruling idea of the building is to make the constructive features aid the ornamentation. The building is constructed of brick with cement dressings. The main front of the building is the concert hall which faces the South . . . The roof is constructed entirely of iron picked out in harmonious colours and the result proves that this very prosaic material can, with judgement, be made to look very effective . . . There are four towers on the structure which give a graceful finish to the fronts of the building'.

The Concert Hall and the Main Hall were each provided with an entrance portico and spacious vestibule. The concert Hall was designed to seat 2800 and was used for dances, concerts and other functions forming part of the every day life of the citizens. But the depression of the 1890s finally forced the takeover of the building by the Queensland Government. As the Museum premises in William Street (now the State Library of Queensland) were proving inadequate, the former Exhibition Building was occupied as the Queensland Museum in 1899. The Queensland Art Gallery moved to the former Concert Hall from the present Land Administration Building in 1930, but moved out again in 1974 as the Gallery once again outgrew its premises. The Queensland Museum moved again in 1986 to its new premises in the Queensland Cultural Centre on the south bank of the Brisbane River. The former Exhibition Building and Concert Hall was subsequently used by the Restaurant and Caterers Association to train young people for work at Expo 88 and in the hospitality and tourist industry generally.

The pipe organ now in the City Hall was originally purchased by the Queensland National Association and installed in the Exhibition Building's Concert Hall.

South Brisbane Town Hall

The Borough of South Brisbane was constituted on 7 January 1888 following agitation by Southsiders, including petitions in 1887, for separation from the North. The original Municipality of Brisbane created in 1859 included both the north and south sides of the river; but in time the river appeared to create a division of interests between the two. The Municipality of South Brisbane subsequently became the South Brisbane Town Council and in 1903 the City of South Brisbane. By November 1890, architects John Hall and Son had completed plans for 'proposed new Municipal Offices at South Brisbane' and construction began early in 1891. The building, which also provided Council Chambers and a 'very convenient and useful public hall' was officially opened on 1 July 1892.

The building is constructed of red bricks said to have come from the Coorparoo brickworks of the builder, Abraham James, and the plain areas of brickwork contrast markedly with the exuberant detail of the ornament executed in sandstone and natural coloured terra cotta.

Construction of the building was not unaccompanied by problems as reflected in the comments of the Mayor who said

The South Brisbane Town Hall, c 1897.

'I feel sure that when the Council are in possession of the new building they will have every reason to be proud of it. Much has been said for and against the erection of these chambers but it must be always understood that when the building was commenced the present state of depression was not existing and once having commenced it was absolutely imperative that the building should be completed, also having in mind that the present chambers are most unsuitable for the Council's requirements'.

On the creation of the Greater Brisbane City Council in 1925, the South Brisbane City Council and others were abolished. Subsequent uses of the former Town Hall included its occupation by the American Army during the Second World War and later by the Conservatorium of Music. It is presently being used as an Adult Education Centre.

On 6 February 1893 Brisbane citizens woke to the news that the northern section of the Victoria Bridge had been washed away by flood-waters. Here they view the remaining southern section from the safety of North Quay.

Even the capital's main street was not safe from the encroaching flood waters. This photo of Queen Street was taken just north of the Edward Street intersection near the G.P.O. Her Majesty's Opera House (near the intersection, centre left) and the Courier Building (right foreground) were completed only a few years earlier, but were recently demolished for redevelopment. Some other buildings visible still exist in 1988.

Flooding in the suburbs — a view towards Hamilton from Jordan Terrace, Bowen Hills, showing the workers' dwellings in the low-lying areas prone to flooding. The Breakfast Creek Hotel is surrounded by flood-waters but Palma Rosa, a grand residence which had only recently been completed, sits safe on its hill in the background.

The 1893 Flood

The year 1893 brought to Brisbane and to other parts of the Colony 'events as extraordinary and practically unknown to present inhabitants of Queensland as they were destructive and calamitous. The first came in the form of a pluvial visitation of extent never before experienced by white residents, which resulted in the inundation of the whole south-eastern corner of the colony'.

Brisbane had experienced its worst flood on record only three years previously when 'following upon a long succession of but briefly broken droughts, which wrought sad havoc among our flocks and agricultural pursuits, Dame Nature, as if ashamed of her neglect, poured rain upon the parched earth in such torrents that the record of the early months is one of terrible floods in all portions of the colony'. Many people believed that the record would remain, even after the rain began in 1893.

Brisbane experienced three floods during February 1893, each in its own right reaching proportions of a major flood. Cyclonic conditions and heavy rains in the latter half of January began the 'real trouble' and by the evening of 3 February Brisbane city was completely isolated. The subsequent events are best described in the 'Review of the Year' for 1893 in *Pugh's Almanac*.

> Crowds lined the high grounds near river banks or wherever a good view was obtainable; and the roar of the water as it rushed along at a speed of from 8 to 10 miles an hour, carrying with it scores of houses, furniture, and household articles in endless variety, together with the whole surrounding scene — formed a combination never to be forgotten. As house after house was carried against Victoria Bridge the crash could be heard over everything, and all that was swept onward was smashed to fragments. The scene on the 5th (Sunday) opened somewhat similar, though the spirit of the people revived somewhat as the thought arose that surely the worst had now passed. But it had not, for about 6 a.m. about one half the Indooroopilly railway bridge, an iron structure which had cost £52,000, was carried away, despite various safeguards adopted, only the southern half remaining erect . . . At about 4 a.m. next morning the Victoria Bridge, spanning the river at Brisbane, met a similar sad fate, as the result of the pressure of accumulated debris against the decking and girders and the weakening of the piers by the long sustained scour . . .

> The steamers and other craft in the Brisbane River had a lively experience, several of them . . . breaking adrift and careering down stream at most hazardous pace . . . [several] were left high and dry in the Botanic Gardens, while the others were deposited ashore at various places between Brisbane and the Bay. Some of them were floated off at the later floods . . . the principal business streets of the city were 15 or 16 feet under water, and all over low lying lands for miles round the suburbs.

> The highest point was reached in Brisbane on the 6th, and as the waters slowly receded active steps were taken by the local authorities to cleanse the city from its deposit of mud and filth . . . Unsettled weather, however, still prevailed, and heavy rains on the 10th and 11th caused a second slight flood in the Brisbane. Another very heavy downpour, which commenced on the 16th and lasted until the 19th, brought down yet a third flood which at 2 p.m. on Sunday (19th) was only 10 inches below that of the 5th and 6th . . . The effects of this third disaster were very similar to the previous calamity, only there were no bridges to carry away, and few houses, those within reach of flood influences having already succumbed.

The northern span of the new Albert Railway Bridge was constructed at the contractors' Indooroopilly site workshop and moved into position by ship.

Indooroopilly Railway Bridge

The 1893 Flood's destruction of the Albert Railway Bridge connecting Indooroopilly and Chelmer was a serious loss. The bridge formed part of the South-Western Railway and the effect of its loss on the carriage of goods, especially for export, was disastrous. Punts and barges helped ease the problem and these became a common site ferrying passengers between these western suburbs.

Henry Charles Stanley was appointed Chief Engineer of Railways for the colony in 1891, and it was on his shoulders fell the responsibility of the design and construction of a new railway bridge at Indooroopilly. Stanley lived in nearby Tighnabruaich and must have had an especial interest in this particular project as his fine home, erected about 1892, stood on high ground above the river and overlooked the bridge site. The magnificent structure which subsequently spanned the river was certainly a credit to Stanley and his accomplishment was described by later admirers as his 'chef d'oeuvre'.

On Saturday, 17 August 1895 Stanley's new bridge was tested successfully, the first engine to cross the bridge being no. 212. At the time, the bridge was the largest in Australia which was 'wholly of local manufacture' — one of the conditions of the contract was that as much of the work as possible should be done in Queensland. A workshop was erected by the contractors at Indooroopilly and thus employment was made possible for a greatly increased number of

men. The largest number employed at any one time was 240 on site, as well as those employed at the quarries.

The bridge consisted of two steel spans, supported on abutments of masonry and a central concrete pier encased in an iron caisson to low water mark and then built up with masonry to the bearings of the girders. Each span was 10.3 m long and each weighed about 610 tonnes. A 'neatly designed footway' was carried on the bridge's upstream side.

Stanley's bridge is still in use today, though with increased traffic and the ultimate electrification of the railway it has been supplemented by an adjacent bridge.

When the first engine crossed the bridge on Saturday, 17 August 1895, it was watched with much interest.

Built to replace the bridge destroyed by the 1893 Flood, the second permanent Victoria Bridge opened in two stages — the downstream section in 1896 and the upstream section in 1897. This bridge in turn was replaced by the present Victoria Bridge. The houses on the south bank are on what is now the site of the Queensland Cultural Centre.

Victoria Bridge, 1897

Jubilee Day, Tuesday, 22 June 1897 was a general holiday throughout Queensland to celebrate the 60th year of the reign of Queen Victoria. Festivities included sports of all kind, tree planting and a grand display of fireworks, but the most significant function, though not the most widely acclaimed at the time, was surely the opening of the new Victoria Bridge by the Governor.

An address was presented to His Excellency on behalf of the Victoria Bridge Board and other citizens, and after the Governor's reply, a procession passed over the bridge to the open square at the southern end which His Excellency named Victoria-place. The procession returned along the upstream half of the bridge to the northern end where the Governor 'descended from his carriage and broke a purple ribbon which was stretched across the bridge and formally declared the structure open'. The downstream section of the bridge had been open to traffic from 1 October 1896.

The bridge was designed by A.B. Brady, Government Architect and Engineer of Bridges, and took three years to complete. It was a steel structure 317 m long, and comprised two carriage ways each 7.3 m wide and two footways each 2.7 m wide. This bridge later was replaced by the present Victoria Bridge and was demolished except for one of the southern entrances which was retained as an historical memorial.

Signal Station, c 1910.

Signal Station

In 1855 Windmill Hill was being considered in relation to the formation of Signal Stations associated with the Electric Telegraph and in 1861 the convict-built Windmill was altered for use as a Semaphore Station. The work, carried out by John Petrie for the Colonial Architect, Charles Tiffin, included 'removing the old arms and wheels with the top and other ponderous timbers inside, laying floors on each storey, putting in new doors and windows and a new weather proof floor on top with Iron railing, a new staircase or ladder from bottom to top, repairing the Stone and Brickwork and plastering . . . and fencing a small triangular plot of ground to make the whole complete'.

An internal winding staircase was installed and a flagstaff was erected 'from which signals will be flying on receipt of shipping news by electric telegraph from Lytton'. A Time Ball was also installed. It was dropped for the first time at 1.00 p.m. on 14 October 1861, providing the inhabitants of Brisbane with 'some reliable authority for the regulation of their clocks and watches'. A Time Gun introduced in June 1866 superceded this Time Ball, but in 1894 a new Time Ball was installed which came into operation officially on 1 January 1895. This copper Time Ball was dropped every day at 1.00 p.m., except Sundays and public holidays, and was in operation until Ocober 1930. It is still visible on top of the building.

For many years from at least the 1880s to the early twentieth century, firemen used the top of the Signal Station as a lookout for fires. The building also was used in the 1920s for radio research work by the Queensland Institute of Radio Engineers and in the 1930s and 1940s for pioneer experimental television broadcasting.

The stone and brick construction, though visible internally, has now been rendered externally (upper half 1861; lower half 1899). The heavy timber beams notched with Roman numerals — probably for ease of construction — are still visible internally and complete the original tower structure. The beams probably formed the base on which the Windmill cap, with sails attached, worked. Though still an interesting landmark, the former Windmill and Signal Station no longer dominates the Brisbane skyline as it did in the nineteenth century. The building is no longer used.

*This illustration of Wickham Terrace appeared in the **Australian Journal** in January 1868 and shows the first Time Ball installed on top of the Signal Station in 1861. The illustration opposite shows the second Time Ball, installed in 1894.*

Aborigines camped on the site of Sedgley Grange in the late 1890s (Above) and the housewarming at Sedgley Grange in 1900 (Opposite). James Trackson, who owned Sedgley Grange, appears in both photos. The plight of the Aborigines is highlighted by the party atmosphere at the Tracksons, the new house accentuates the primitive nature of the 'gunyah' and the fine clothes of the party-goers contrast with the 'cast-offs' worn by the Aborigines.

Cultural Contrasts and Unevenness of Development

The transformation of Brisbane by the turn of the century had taken place so rapidly that it was characterised by marked contrasts and unevenness of development.

Many of the grand buildings erected in the city in the 1880s were neighbours still to single storey shanties. Suburban development during the 1880s and improved transport services enticed people further from the inner city area and commuters became neighbours to agriculturalists and to a few remaining Aborigines.

Relationships between the Europeans and the local Aborigines had been a mixture of good and bad depending mainly on individual attitudes and experiences, but by the

1890s the local Aborigines had been reduced mainly to 'figures of curiosity, occasional charity and derision'.

The contrasts of the two cultures were highlighted at Alderley, where some of the Enoggera tribe still survived in the late 1890s close to where James Trackson built his new residence, Sedgley Grange. Their primitive gunyah and their cast-off clothes, for example, contrasted markedly with the new home erected by James Trackson and the fine clothes worn by his family and visitors. The gunyah was described by German missionary, Christopher Eipper, in 1844 as being easy to construct 'as they have only to fix three sticks in the form of a triangle in the ground, and to cover them with the bark of the tea-tree. Their hut, when complete, assumes the form of a bee-hive cut asunder in the middle, and is from three to four feet in width, and six in diameter; the floor being covered with a piece of the same bark, upon which they lie down, in the only position which the shape of the hut will allow of, namely, with the body bent into a semi-circle'.

The two cultures were contrasted further when the railway reached Enoggera in 1899 and James Trackson had built his own steam car by the following year — the first privately owned car to be driven on Brisbane streets. Trackson, of the firm of Trackson Brothers, was very interested in early cars, experimenting with various types which he kept at Sedgley Grange.

heat. As with the Japanese, the proper method of making a house cool here is to "take down the walls," not, as in those regions of Australia where hot winds prevail, to close the house against the blast. In the coast districts of Queensland, evening on a verandah were, but for the mosquitoes, existence worthy a lotus-eater. By usage it is at all times a drawing-room, and often bears the dancing-floor of the house. Many of these pretty, cool dwellings peep from among the trees or show out upon the hill-sides round Brisbane, where in time to come they will be thickly dotted'.

Woodlands was built at Ashgrove in the 1890s. French doors open onto wide surrounding verandahs with cast iron balustrades and protective venetian blinds. 'Evening on a verandah were, but for the mosquitoes, existence worthy a lotus-eater'.

Hillcrest at Taringa (built c 1890) is a timber house with low windows opening onto surrounding verandahs which are now protected by both lattice and venetians.

Architecture of Brisbane Dwelling Houses

The architecture of Brisbane houses has attracted attention for approximately a century and its interesting features were described by an anonymous writer in 1888.

'One of the first features which strike the attention of the stranger approaching Brisbane, especially by the river, is the architecture of the dwelling-houses. The prevailing style is, with modifications, that of the Indian bungalow — a single, sometimes double, storeyed cottage, generally of wood, with pyramidal roof, and surrounded by broad verandahs, upon which open many French doors or low windows. Closed in by bamboo curtains or Venetians, furnished with hammocks, ample cane lounges and easy-chairs, the verandah is on summer evenings the most important tributary to the comfort of a house. By keeping off the heat of the sun's rays from windows and walls, it enables the house to be kept cool and open to the sea-breeze, which, blowing from the north-east, is the great temperer of the summer

A recent view of Glengariff at Hendra, former home of the late T.C. Beirne.

Glengariff

One of the most prominent figures in Brisbane's commercial history was T.C. Beirne, who arrived in Australia in 1884 at the age of 24, after realising his bleak future prospects in impoverished Ireland. At Beirne's death on 21 April 1949, the *Courier-Mail* reported that 'Brisbane has lost a personality whose life has been woven strongly into its own progress and development for half a century. He attained commercial eminence although born in circumstances that permitted only an elementary education. He was successful also in politics, in public life, and finance'.

Beirne was a benefactor of the University of Queensland and of several other educational and charitable institutions, was Warden of the University, a member of the Legislative Council of the Queensland Parliament, and was awarded a Papal Knighthood of the Order of St Gregory for his work for the Catholic church. But Beirne is probably best remembered in association with his Valley department store, now David Jones Limited.

In the late 1890s a large residence at Hendra became T.C. Beirne's home, which he named Glengariff after a picturesque locality in southern Ireland. Beirne lived here until his death when his five daughters, who had spent such pleasant times at Glengariff and 'could not bear to sell the place', gave it to the Catholic Church as a residence for the Co-adjutor Archbishop.

Glengariff is similar to the homes of many other successful merchants throughout Australia and is characterised by a brick structure complete with entry tower, a large double height bay window, and an elegant two storey cast iron verandah overlooking formal lawns.

Rhyndarra, c 1914. Built as a private residence, it later became a Salvation Army home for girls, and is now the Officers' Quarters and Mess at the Yeronga Military Hospital.

Rhyndarra

A large two storey stone and brick residence was completed at Yeronga in 1889 for William Williams, who was manager of the Australasian Steam Navigation Company prior to the formation of the A.U.S.N. Company and later became the financial agent for the Australian Mutual Provident Society. Rhyndarra was designed by the Italian architect Andrea Stombuco and was situated above the Brisbane River with the main facade facing towards the Oxley Plains. 'Except for the two bow windows, which with their gabled roof project beyond the main house, the verandahs and balconies would quite encompass the house. These bows make a pleasing break in the otherwise uniform front of the building . . .'.

The home was provided with separate servants' quarters, kitchen and dairy, and cellars were constructed below.

Williams was very fond of horses and ran them and a herd of dairy cows on his property. The fine brick stables erected for him still exist.

Williams appears to have fallen on hard times and left Rhyndarra, which he had mortgaged to the A.M.P. Society, in the late 1890s. In 1897 the Salvation Army opened a home for girls at Rhyndarra, which became a 'blessed and sacred spot to many young girls who in the hour of orphanhood or danger have been taken into the arms of love and maternal care'. The property was subdivided in 1907.

During the Second World War the Rhyndarra property was taken over by the Armed Forces and developed as a Military Hospital which it remains today. It was acquired by the Commonwealth in October 1946 and the former residence in now the Officers' Mess and Quarters.

"Attow's Pineapple Plantation near Nudgee — loading for market", c 1897.

Pineapple Growing and the Northgate Cannery

'Much of the cultivation near Brisbane is not interesting as a feature of the landscape, but the novelty of some of the productions commands attention. Maize, sugar-cane and pine-apple fields, especially the last, are calculated to puzzle the stranger only accustomed to the crops of temperate climes. The pine-apple is a crop of egregious appearance. The pine-apple is composed of a bunch of smooth blade-like leaves, about eighteen inches or two feet in length, of a purplish green tint and armed with sharp saw edges and hard point. These leaves spring from a common centre, rising in a circle from a small base at the root, and spread out in graceful curves round the fruit which springs from a stalk in their midst, and itself bears a crown of smaller leaves, like those of the plant, smooth of surface and serrated of edge. The fruit, as it swells and ripens, turns from a dusty green to different tints of yellow, according to the species. The plants are grown in rows, a foot or so apart, and rise not more than two feet from the ground'. Thus the humble pineapple was described in *Picturesque Australasia* in 1888.

Introduced into Australia during the nineteenth century, pineapples have always formed an important part of Brisbane's local produce. In October 1947 the Golden Circle Cannery at Northgate was opened and today is the largest individual fruit cannery in Australia and perhaps the Southern Hemisphere. It was originally planned as a pineapple cannery but its operations have diversified to cater for all varieties of fruits and vegetables supplied for processing by Queensland growers.

85

Proclamation of the Commonwealth of Australia, 1 January 1901

The Commonwealth Bill received Royal assent on 9 July 1900 and 'the opening of the twentieth century', 1 January 1901, was decided upon as the date for the proclamation of the establishment of the Commonwealth.

On 19 September 1900 it was announced that the Duke of York would open the first Commonwealth Parliament in Melbourne in March 1901; and subsequently it was announced that 'a body of troops representing all British arms' would be present at the inauguration celebrations on 1 January 1901. The Governor-General, Lord Hopetoun, arrived in Sydney on 10 December 1900 and the Imperial troops arrived a few days later. Both received magnificent receptions.

On 1 January 1901, the inauguration of the Australian Commonwealth was celebrated in Brisbane by a series of public functions which lasted from 9.00 a.m. to 10.00 p.m. The Governor, Lord Chelmsford, read the proclamation from a balcony of the imposing Treasury Building which was bedecked with bunting and palm leaves, reflecting this auspicious but happy occasion.

The Governor of Queensland, Lord Chelmsford, read the proclamation of the Commonwealth of Australia from a balcony of the Treasury Building overlooking William Street.

The Commonwealth Procession passing down Queen Street towards Albert Street. (The buildings in the right foreground still exist. The tall building on the left, with decorative cast iron lacework, is the Carlton Hotel).

The Commonwealth Procession, 17 January 1901

The visit of the Imperial troops to Brisbane was eagerly looked forward to — many of those people born in Australia had never witnessed spectacular displays of large bodies of troops. The city was decorated with arches, pennants, flags, greenery, etc. and was brilliantly lit at night. The troops, numbering about 1200, arrived by ship on 16 January and were accorded a splendid reception the following day, greeted by tens of thousands of Queenslanders who thronged the streets of the capital. The *Orient* also had arrived in Moreton Bay the same day as the Imperial troops, returning members of the First Contingent from the Boer War, and there were also about 1500 'local troops' in Brisbane at the time.

The Imperial troops departed on 19 January and on 20 January a thanksgiving service was held in St John's Pro-Cathedral for the safe return of the members of the First Contingent.

At the outbreak of war in South Africa, the Queensland Government had offered to send troops to assist the British against the Boers — the first Australian colony to make such an offer, or as *Pugh's Almanac* stated in 1901 'the first colony wherein the spirit of loyalty and military ardour took practical form in offering assistance to the mother country in the shape of men and arms'. On 1 November 1899, the First Contingent of Queensland troops bound for the Transvaal had embarked on the S.S. *Cornwall* at Pinkenba.

87

presented arms and the band rang out the National Anthem, Lord Chelmsford removed the covering from the statue'. At the same time the Royal Standard was hoisted on the flag pole attached to the platform and before the music ceased Lady Chelmsford placed a wreath containing orchids and violets on the statue's granite and freestone pedestal. The *Brisbane Courier* explained the significance of the event, stating that the statue 'perpetuates the memory of one whose great care was her people's good, who set the nation an example as wife and mother, the lustre of whose womanhood served to purify the social life, the literature and the art of the Victorian era'.

When the Governor of Queensland, Lord Chelmsford, unveiled the bronze statue of Queen Victoria in 1906, the recently completed Executive Building formed an imposing background.

The Executive Gardens c 1910, with the Executive Building (now the Land Administration Building) at the left and the former State Library, previously Queensland Museum, in the background.

Unveiling of the Statue of Queen Victoria in the Executive Gardens, 23 June 1906

A new building was erected by the Queensland Government during the years 1901–05, overlooking what is now Queen's Park. It was referred to in the early years of construction as the 'New Lands and Survey Offices', but towards the time of completion became known as the Executive Building. The second floor housed the Premier's offices, his Under Secretary, officials of the Public Service Board and the 'Cabinet Room', whilst on the third floor, a 'large room facing the whole length of the George Street front is allotted to the Trustees of the Queensland National Art Gallery for the collection of works of art'.

The building (now the Land Administration Building) was entirely faced with stone — granite for the base, course and plinth, with freestone above — and was erected on the site of Brisbane's first electric telegraph office and the former convict settlement's parsonage, later the commissariat officers' quarters.

The gardens established adjacent to the building after the demolition of St John's Pro-Cathedral were initially known as the Executive Gardens. On 23 June 1906 a bronze statue of Queen Victoria, a replica by Thomas Brock of the original in Portsmouth, was unveiled by the Governor. 'As the troops

Now part of St Peter's Lutheran College at Indooroopilly, Ross Roy was formerly a well known private residence and was featured in the **Queensland Society Magazine** *in the 1920s.*

Ross Roy

When Queensland pastoralist and pioneer William Ross Munro decided to retire from the land, he left the choice of location to his wife. Ross Munro, as he was known, was nearing sixty. He had been born on 20 February 1850, about 15 miles from the present town of Narrabri in New South Wales. He acquired a love of the land from his father, who was an inspiration to his children but died at the age of 48.

Ross Munro had his 'ups and downs' as a pioneer pastoralist but his Scottish shrewdness and good judgment, 'his breeding and instinctive precepts', helped him to success.

Mrs Munro chose Brisbane for their retirement and as their home, a magnificent two storey residence on a hilltop at Indooroopilly, overlooking the Brisbane River to Yeerongpilly and Archerfield beyond. The big brick home was surrounded by decorative though functional verandahs at both levels and was called Ross Roy. Mrs Munro, a garden lover, had the poor soil at Ross Roy supplemented and the gardens which were developed soon became much admired. In the 1920s the house was featured twice in the *Queensland Society Magazine.*

Mrs Munro died in 1938 and Ross Munro died in May 1944, aged 94. In November 1944, Ross Roy was sold to the Lutheran Church authorities and St Peters Lutheran College, now one of Brisbane's leading schools, was subsequently established there.

Meeting of the Automobile Club, April 1908.

James Trackson and Mrs Trackson in the Steam Locomobile, the first motor car in Brisbane, in front of Trackson Brothers office in 1902.

First Cars in Brisbane

The first privately owned car to be driven on Brisbane's streets appeared in 1900. It was a steam car built by James Trackson and it was received with mixed feelings by the local community, some of whom believed it should be kept off the streets in the interests of public safety. But within a few years motoring had become a favourite 'sport' and provided the means of many pleasant outings. Automobile clubs were formed and motor rallies became popular. The subsequent success of the motor car needs no further comment.

Sandgate

Sandgate was surveyed in 1852 and on 22 March 1853 the *New South Wales Government Gazette* included notification that a site had been 'fixed for a village at . . . Sandgate, at Cabbage Tree Head, in the District of Moreton Bay'. The first land sales there took place later in the year.

By the 1880s Sandgate had grown into a pleasant residential area and on 29 April 1880 was proclaimed a town. The railway from Roma Street was opened in May 1882 and it became a popular nearby seaside resort for Brisbane people visiting by rail or road. By 1887 there was a 'pier of no mean pretensions for the accommodation of visitors from the capital; the Corporation . . . has also greatly improved the facilities for bathing, by erecting several public bathing-houses and shelter-sheds. With these and other attractions' said Cassell's *Picturesque Australasia* 'it is not so surprising that the place should be so largely resorted to by the citizens of Brisbane, pining for breezes that are as the breath of life to lungs which, in the heated air of the capital, have almost forgotten their office'.

In 1906 the *Australasian Handbook* described Sandgate as 'a favourite resort for enthusiastic fishermen and boating parties, a large number of yachts being kept by residents and others . . . A Town Band performs in the parks frequently during the summer evenings, special excursion trains being run from Brisbane . . . The accommodation for visitors has been much improved by the erection of public bathing-houses and several shelter sheds by the Corporation'. Sandgate's main park was Moora Park adjoining the pier, which afforded fine views of the bay from its high ground above the cliffs.

In 1925 Sandgate was incorporated into Greater Brisbane and no longer had its own council. It is now a residential suburb of Brisbane.

'Sandgate by the sea', c 1910.

Fernberg—Government House

The present Government House was built as a private residence for John Christian Heussler, merchant and politician, who acquired the magnificent elevated site at Bardon in the early 1860s. Heussler called his home 'Fernberg', a word of German origin meaning the 'distant mountain'. The view of the city suburbs and district from Fernberg, set in its own magnificent park-like gardens, were 'something out of the common, both for extent, variety and beauty'.

Additions and alterations were later made to Fernberg to give its present classic Italianate appearance, probably when the then owner, John Stevenson, visited Scotland in 1889.

When the Queensland Government was seeking an alternative to Government House in George Street in 1909, Fernberg was eventually chosen as a temporary residence for the Governor who moved there in June 1910. The home and grounds were purchased in 1911 and Fernberg became the Governor's official permanent residence.

A view in Albion c 1910, looking towards Donatello, now part of St Margaret's School. Note the quarries in the background and the chimneys of the potteries and brickworks.

St Margaret's and Suburban Albion

The suburb of Albion began as a strange mixture of settlement — the large imposing residences built on its choice hilltop positions contrasted markedly with the brickworks, potteries, quarries, mills and other enterprises established in the area, including those of the Petrie and Campbell families who lived nearby. The development of the area owed much to these two families who lived at Mooloomburrum and Donatello respectively, and who became linked by marriage as well as by St Margaret's School at Albion.

Donatello, formerly Roslyn, was one of Brisbane's imposing early private homes. It is now Community House, part of St Margaret's School, having been purchased by the

Sisters of the Sacred Advent in 1910 for what was then their Eton High School. They had moved a few years previously from their original premises at Nundah to Toorak House on the Hamilton Heights, which they leased, but they found it 'too great a climb for day pupils'. Donatello was 'situated on the heights at Albion' and was considered 'just as airy and healthy as Toorak but much more accessible . . . being within three minutes walk of the Clayfield tramline'.

The name of Donatello was changed to St Margaret's House and the school was subsequently known as the Church of England High School for Girls. The school has expanded considerably since then and, amongst other things, has acquired Mooloomburrum, the former residence of Andrew Petrie, adjacent to Donatello.

A recent view of the People's Palace which is lavishly decorated with three tiers of cast iron lacework.

The People's Palace

One of the few remaining large corner hotels in Brisbane, lavishly decorated with cast iron lacework, the People's Palace was opened by the Salvation Army on 27 June 1911. Its elevated position above the city centre, close to Central Station, was justifiably claimed to be 'in itself an advantage, as the business-like Salvation Army officers who will manage it expect to entertain many of the travelling public'. The building included a large roof garden — 'the highest in Brisbane' — verandahs with ornate cast iron decoration and a polygonal corner tower overlooking the intersection of Ann and Edward Streets. Cheap accommodation 'but no liquor bar' was offered at the 'Palace' by the Salvation Army until May 1979. The building was subsequently leased to a private operator, but it is now Salvation Army headquarters.

Sacred Heart Church and Convent of Mercy, Rosalie

For many years the Catholics who settled at suburban Rosalie were without their own local church and travelled to nearby St Brigid's at Red Hill. A small timber church was built at Rosalie in the 1890s, on a site believed to have been purchased at the first land sales in the area. This church was replaced within ten years and on 17 June 1917 the foundation stone for a third church was laid by Archbishop Duhig.

The new Sacred Heart Church at Rosalie was dedicated by the Apostolic Delegate, Monsignor Cattaneo, on 16 June 1918. An impressive brick structure, it was designed by prominent Brisbane architect G.H.M. Addison in Romanesque style and was described at the time of its opening as 'one of the most

handsome Parish Churches in the Commonwealth'. A presbytery was erected nearby in 1914.

The Convent of Mercy was added to the group in 1918. Designed by the architect T.R. Hall, this fine ecclesiastical building was well suited to the local climate, its wide surrounding verandahs with decorative timberwork providing protection from both sun and rain whilst still allowing the flow of cooling breezes. A matching fence in brick with decorative timber finish forms an attractive foreground to the building.

The Sacred Heart Church (Above) and the Convent of Mercy (Left) were designed by prominent Brisbane architects and form part of an interesting though loosely connected group of church buildings at Rosalie, including a Presbytery and a school.

Anzac Day, Brisbane, 1916.

BEING THE FIRST ANNIVERSARY OF THE MEMORABLE LANDING OF AUSTRALASIAN TROOPS ON THE GALLIPOLI PENINSULA, 25th APRIL, 1915, OPERATING AGAINST THE GERMAN-TURKISH ARMY IN THE GREAT WAR OF EMPIRES

Saluting Base of the Military Parade, opposite the General Post Office.

First Anzac Day

On the first Anzac Day, 25 April 1916, a message from His Majesty King George V, addressed to the people of Australia, was published throughout Queensland by command of the Governor, Sir Hamilton Goold-Adams. This message said to 'tell my people of Australia that today I am joining with them in their solemn tribute to the memory of their heroes who died in Gallipoli. They gave their lives for a supreme cause in gallant comradeship with the rest of my sailors and soldiers who fought and died with them. Their valour and fortitude have shed fresh lustre on the British Arms. May those who mourn their loss find comfort in the conviction that they did not die in vain, but that their sacrifice has drawn our peoples more closely together and added strength and glory to the Empire'.

The Anzacs gave honour to their country before the eyes of the world. The hardship and danger they suffered against all odds developed the legend of Australian 'mateship', endurance and equality that is remembered as the 'spirit of Anzac'. The anniversary of the landing of the Anzacs in the dark at Gallipoli and the storming of the heights has become a national day in Australia, symbolising the comradeship, courage, tenacity and sacrifice of those who have fought and died that we, the succeeding generations, might live and enjoy the great opportunities offering in Australia today.

Anzac Square

Following the First World War, there was a strong feeling throughout the population to commemorate the ANZACS and their efforts by the construction of a memorial, and subscriptions to a War Memorial Fund were collected throughout Queensland from the early 1920s. By 1924 proposals for an Anzac Memorial Square were crystallizing and a competition for a suitable design was won by the architects Buchanan and Cowper.

The design comprised a lower level park containing radial pathways focusing on an upper level Shrine — an eternal flame located at the centre of a rotunda of Doric columns supporting a circular entablature. Bottle trees for the park were donated by Colonel Cameron, Member of the House of Representatives for Brisbane at the time of the Anzac Square proposals, in memory of the Light Horse Regiments with which he served.

The public dedication ceremony was held on Remembrance Day, 11 November 1930. The architects, commenting on this memorial just prior to its dedication, said that 'to visitors near and far the site and setting of the Anzac Square Memorial will appear unique and, from every point of view, its environment will be proclaimed as picturesque and in harmony with the most meritorious of the many memorials raised throughout the British Empire to express the Empire's desire and determination to honour and remember its soldiers'.

Views of Anzac Square from the Shrine (Below) and towards the Shrine (Above).

Saint Martin's Memorial Hospital Building

Saint Martin's was built as a War Memorial Hospital and in launching the appeal for it in the *Church Chronicle* of 1 May 1919, Archbishop Donaldson said that 'it seems right, then, that both as an art of Thanksgiving and as an expression of our undying remembrance of those who have died for us, we should bestir ourselves to erect a worthy memorial to which future generations may look as a record of our conflict and trial'.

The foundation stone was laid by the Governor of Queensland, Sir Hamilton Goold-Adams, on 9 November 1919 — just two days less than a year after the signing of the Armistice. Three years later, on 28 November 1922, the hospital was opened by the Governor–General of Australia, Baron Forster. It was designed by the architect Lange Powell in a style typical of seventeenth century Renaissance, with a little of the Jacobean and Gothic, 'the whole being thoroughly English . . . at the same time . . . to harmonize it with the climatic conditions of our State, and more particularly to produce a result that would be in proper and decent feeling with the very beautiful Cathedral — to group up both buildings to form a harmonious whole'.

Saint Martin's is a truly beautiful building overall, and its detailing is superb. The latter includes cruciform rain-water spouts and a statue of Saint Martin of Tours in a niche in the western gable.

The building is presently used as cathedral offices, choir vestries etc., and as the Precentor's residence.

Above: *A quiet courtyard formed between Saint Martin's Hospital Building and Saint John's Cathedral provided a welcome retreat for the former hospital's recuperating patients. It contains a stone memorial to Bishop Le Fanu, the Bishop Co-adjutor of Brisbane at the time of construction of Saint Martin's.*

Left: *Saint Martin's was carefully designed to harmonize with and enhance the adjacent Saint John's Cathedral. Constructed of brick and sandstone, with a terracotta shingle tiled roof, its design is a 'sophisticated assembly of motifs' and shows similarities to English architect Philip Webb's famous Red House (1859) in the conical roof of the minor operating theatre, apex vents, finials, chimneys, tiles and windows.*

Saint John's Cathedral

The foundation stone for the first stage of Saint John's Cathedral was laid in 1901 by the Duke and Duchess of York, later King George V and Queen Mary. The design of this fine Gothic Revival cathedral was by the English architect J. Pearson and the architectural impact is achieved mainly by the lofty interior supported on tall delicately proportioned columns, the low level of lighting and the colonnades. The plan is a traditional cross, with a double aisle either side of the nave and chapels and an ambulatory flanking the sanctuary.

The cathedral is unfinished, being erected in stages, the first of which was consecrated on 28 October 1910. The exterior is of Brisbane tuff or porphyry whilst the interior is of freestone. The cathedral stands on the cliff above Adelaide Street, between the Deanery and Saint Martin's Hospital Building. A quiet courtyard is formed between the cathedral and Saint Martin's, and the latter protects the cathedral from the noise and visual intrusion of the city below and to the south-east. Saint John's is reputedly one of the finest Gothic cathedrals in the Southern Hemisphere.

Above: *The lofty interior of Brisbane's Anglican Cathedral with its tall, delicately proportioned columns, its low level of lighting and its colonnades, contributes to Saint John's reputation as one of the finest Gothic cathedrals in the Southern Hemisphere.*

Right: *Saint John's Cathedral was erected adjacent to Adelaide House, the initial home of Queensland's first Governor and now the Deanery of Saint John's. Adelaide House is at the extreme right of this picture. Saint Martin's was erected on the opposite side of the Cathedral, on the site of the residence at the left of the picture. The buildings stand above a steep cliff excavated in the late nineteenth century for the smooth continuation of Adelaide Street.*

"MERCURY SERIES" 19. BRISBANE. St. JOHN'S ANGLICAN CATHEDRAL.

Residences Designed by Robin Dods

One of Brisbane's architects with a particularly distinctive and significant style was Robin Dods, whose domestic architectural prowess has been described as 'creating "stylistic elegance" out of the crude "Brisbane Vernacular" '.

Dods took the forms that were associated with the traditional Brisbane domestic architecture and incorporated them as part of his design language. Prior to this, buildings of any pretence to 'quality' were built in a style reminiscent of European models.

Dods's houses, for example, show careful detailing of the verandah and entry, with a feeling of Art Nouveau/Queen Anne style. However, Dods did not admire all aspects of the Queensland vernacular and in many houses he screened the stumps from view by extending the weatherboards to ground level.

Blair Lodge

Upon the high ground flanking the Brisbane River as it flows through the suburbs, there are many fine homes with spacious verandahs enabling semi-outdoor enjoyment of views and prevailing breezes, whilst providing protection from sun and rain.

Blair Lodge is a well known landmark overlooking the river at Hamilton. Built just after the turn of the century, it shows the delight of the designer in producing a complex roof with projecting dormers above a verandah thrust out towards the view and supported above the steep slope by tall lattice enclosed stumps.

The Paddock at Ascot Racecourse in 1928.

Ascot Racecourse

The early settlers needed to relax occasionally and sports meetings of the day were well attended. Horse racing was conducted periodically in various parts of Brisbane, but on 3 August 1863 a meeting of fifty-three 'prominent gentlemen' formed the Queensland Turf Club, which thereafter firmly established racing as a regular sport in Brisbane. A government grant of 130 ha of land at Eagle Farm was made to the Club and the first meeting was held on 14 August 1865. The course was 'right handed oval, one mile and a half in length, with a quarter of a mile straight run in. It is flat and nearly cleared of timber'.

It was recorded that 'owners, jockeys, trainers, hangers-on and the flotsam and jetsam of the sporting community at that time all had a hand in mapping out and clearing the land to shape it into a semblance of a racecourse. The course was originally one and a-half miles, but later on reduced to one mile and a few yards, and the lagoon, of which there is hardly a vestige left, occupied a fair area in the centre, and, when Jupiter Pluvius paid a visitation at the particular time the races were held, the best mud horse always came out on top, and the public — more particularly the judges — had great difficulty in distinguishing their various fancies when they reached the winning post . . .

'From the very primitive spot it was in the early '60's, the Eagle Farm reserve has been transformed into one of the most up-to-date and most picturesque racecourses in Australia. Leading southern owners and trainers who have visited Brisbane in recent years have publicly stated that the course proper at Eagle Farm has no equal in Australia as a racing track. And what could be more picturesque or beautiful than the general surroundings of Eagle Farm, more particularly its saddling paddock . . .

'The grandstands and other buildings are complete with the most modern appointments and conveniences, and are more than capable of coping with present day requirements, but the Q.T.C. Committee of the day is a progressive body, and looking to the future has made arrangements for further additions and improvements, which will add much to the requirements of future generations'.

*Cover illustration from **Souvenir of the laying of the first stone of the Holy Name Cathedral**, 1928.*

On Sunday, 16 September 1928 Cardinal Cerretti, 'surrounded by the most numerous and brilliant assemblage that has ever marked a Catholic religious function in Brisbane', laid the foundation stone for the new cathedral. In a newspaper article in 1935, Archbishop Duhig described events after the completion of the foundations:

> Before the work of raising the superstructure could be gone on with it was necessary to arrange for the supply of building material. On the recommendation of the architect, and an eminent Sydney engineer, it was decided to use Benedict Stone. This entailed the obtaining of rights to manufacture the stone in Australia and the erection of extensive workshops and machinery for the purpose. After many months of search for a suitable location for the works, the site alongside the railway at Light Street, Bowen Hills was purchased, and the machinery, which had been imported from America, was duly installed.

> Before, however, much production could be gone on with, Queensland was in the grip of the depression and the work of building the Cathedral had to be postponed indefinitely. However notwithstanding the bad times, contributions never ceased to pour in, and, encouraged by the revival of prosperity and the loyal support of our priests and people, I determined nine months ago to complete the crypt and open it for public worship.

> Since the laying of the foundation stone of the Cathedral no less a sum than £100,000 has been contributed towards the erection of the building. About £80,000 of this has been spent on the actual work of the Cathedral, and about £20,000 on the Benedict Stone Works to provide material. The completion and furnishing of the crypt is costing about £9,000, but more generous support than ever is being received from the people, who are all delighted at the prospect of seeing this first portion of the Cathedral opened for public worship. The erection of the main building will be gone on with as funds become available, and, with God's blessing, will be completed at no very distant date.

The Foundation Stone and Crypt of the Proposed Holy Name Cathedral

The site for the future Holy Name Cathedral was purchased by Archbishop Sir James Duhig in 1915 from the City Council, who had intended it for a future Town Hall. The site was previously that of the Archbishop's residence, Dara. Plans for the cathedral were prepared by the architects Hennessy and Hennessy of Sydney and on 9 June 1927 three sods were turned on the site, one by the Mayor, W.A. Jolly, another by T.C. Beirne and the third by Archbishop Duhig. After excavations for the building began, the Archbishop left for Rome to arrange the laying of the foundation stone by the Apostolic Delegate who was to visit Australia the following year.

The crypt was opened in August 1935 but construction of the superstructure has never eventuated. The site was recently sold by the Catholic Church.

Opposite: *The City Hall clock tower rises majestically skywards overlooking the recently reconstructed City Square.*

Above: *Inside the main auditorium of the City Hall, 14 July 1931. The city organ in the background was originally installed in the Exhibition Concert Hall (later the Queensland Museum).*

Brisbane City Hall

For many years dissatisfaction had been felt with the Town Hall erected in Queen Street in the 1860s and there were agitations for the erection of a new building. Finally, the present City Hall was constructed and was officially opened on 8 April 1930 by the Governor of Queensland, Sir John Goodwin. The building had two foundation stones, the first laid at the Ann Street corner in 1917 by the Governor, Sir Hamilton Goold-Adams, and the second laid at the Adelaide Street corner on 29 July 1920 by H.R.H. the Prince of Wales, later King Edward VIII.

The building was designed by the Brisbane architects Hall & Prentice and covered an island site of over two acres. The building was planned axially about a circular concert hall with a copper dome, and administrative offices occupied the space between the hall and the rectangular perimeter. Ionic colonnades extended either side of the central main entrance portico with a pediment above containing a sculpture by Daphne Mayo, 16 m long, depicting the settlement of Queensland by the early pioneers. A magnificent clock tower rose 91 m above street level, dominating the building and overlooking the city.

The fine city organ, built by Henry Willis and Sons, of London, was removed from the Exhibition Concert Hall and installed in the new City Hall. The opportunity was taken to completely overhaul and improve the organ which, it was believed, 'was now one of the best in the Southern Hemisphere'.

The City Hall today is still one of Brisbane's finest buildings and has been undergoing restoration over the past few years. A Civic Art Gallery and Museum, of a high standard, has also been established in this building which belongs to the citizens of Brisbane.

Early Days of Qantas

The idea of Qantas was conceived just after the First World War when, in 1919, two young ex-Royal Flying Corps Lieutenants, P.J. McGuiness and W. Hudson Fysh, were surveying the route of the England to Australia Air Race in an old Model T Ford. A prize of $20 000 was being offered by the Australian Government for the first Australian to fly from England to Australia within 28 days. Whilst Fysh and McGuiness were battling the rugged inland in their Ford, they became convinced that an air service should be established to encourage development of the isolated Australian outback.

On 16 November 1920 the Queensland and Northern Territory Aerial Service was registered and for many years the headquarters were located at Longreach in central western Queensland. Whilst here, Qantas established the first regular air mail service in Queensland (November 1922), built its own aircraft (from 1925), operated flying schools at Longreach and at Brisbane, helped in flood rescue work and other emergency operations in the outback, and provided the sole flying facilities for many years for the Flying Doctor Service.

On 17 April 1929 a service between Brisbane and Charleville was opened by Qantas, thus completing its service from north-western Queensland to Brisbane, and in June 1930 Qantas moved its headquarters to Brisbane (Eagle Farm). It had just completed its first 1 000 000 miles flown. In January 1932 the headquarters moved to Archerfield Aerodrome — 'the old Eagle Farm aerodrome had been abandoned, much against our will, by the Civil Aviation Authority, owing to the heavy expense of extensions over swampy ground'. (It was later developed by the Americans during the Second World War and has now become the main domestic and international terminal in Queensland.)

The involvement of Qantas in experimental mail services between England and Australia in 1931 foreshadowed the establishment of a regular service in December 1934 and the ultimate expansion of Qantas internationally. On 18 January 1934 Qantas Empire Airways was registered and in 1967 it became Qantas Airways Ltd. Qantas is now wholly owned by the Australian Government.

*This photograph of Q.A.N.T.A.S. at Archerfield Aerodrome appeared in the **Queenslander** on 25 January 1934, after the Eagle Farm Aerodrome had been abandoned by the Civil Aviation Authorities.*

*Kingsford-Smith's **Southern Cross** on display at Brisbane Airport.*

Sir Charles Kingsford-Smith and the *Southern Cross*

Charles Kingsford-Smith or 'Smithy' as he became known, was born in Brisbane in 1897 and later worked with the Colonial Sugar Refining Company. During the First World War he joined the First A.I.F. and served in Egypt, Gallipoli and France, and was selected to join the Royal Flying Corps, where he won the Military Cross. After the war he flew as a stunt and joy-ride pilot in Britain, America and Australia, in 1922 he joined the first commercial company to operate in Australia, West Australian Airways, and he became a pioneer of flying in New Guinea.

With Charles Ulm, Kingsford-Smith flew around Australia in a D.H. Moth in 1927 and in June 1928 the pair, together with Americans Harry Lyon as navigator and James Warner as radio operator, flew across the Pacific in a three-engined Fokker, the *Southern Cross* — the first trans-Pacific flight in history. The two (in the *Southern Cross*) were the first to fly the Tasman Sea to New Zealand and over the Atlantic from Ireland to Newfoundland. Kingsford-Smith flew solo from England to Australia in 1930 in a record breaking time for those days of 9 days 21 hours and 40 minutes.

Kingsford-Smith continued as a record-breaking pilot and in 1934 flew the Pacific from Australia to San Francisco with P.G. Taylor in the *Lady Southern Cross*, a single engine plane — one of his finest flights. On 8 November 1935, whilst attempting a record flight from England to Australia with aviation mechanic Tommy Pethybridge, he disappeared in his Lockheed Altair aircraft about 320 km south of Rangoon.

Kingsford-Smith was knighted in 1932 for his services to aviation. The *Southern Cross* was acquired by the Commonwealth Government in 1935 and is now on display in a memorial building at the entrance to Brisbane Airport (Eagle Farm), where its first landing in Australia was made by Kingsford-Smith at the completion of the trans-Pacific flight in 1928.

Crowds at the official opening of the Grey Street Bridge on 30 March 1932.

Opening the Grey Street (William Jolly) Bridge

On 31 March 1932 the *Queenslander* reported that 'while the magnificent pageant which marked the ceremonial opening of the Sydney Harbour Bridge only 10 days before distracted the general attraction from the more modest celebration arranged for the new bridge over the Brisbane River from Grey Street to North Quay . . . the function of yesterday, when his Excellency Sir John Goodwin declared the bridge open for public use, created a great deal of local interest'.

The bridge was built of reinforced concrete with the surface treated 'to make it resemble light-coloured porphyry rather than the ordinary cement plaster with which buildings are faced'. The new bridge was what was known as the rainbow arch type and was said to be the first of its kind in Australia and to the best knowledge of the designer, A.E.

Harding Frew, the first of this type in the world in which more than one span had been attempted. The contractors, M.R. Hornibrook Ltd, officially began work by the laying of a datum block by the then Mayor of Brisbane, William Jolly, after whom the bridge is now named.

This bridge was designed to relieve congestion of traffic on Victoria Bridge during the busy hours, but as the *Queenslander* reported at the time of its opening, 'there was much difference of opinion as to whether this object will be attained in view of the out-of-the-way position of the new cross-river bridge . . . However, the controversy on this point has dwindled away of late, a proposal for yet another bridge from Bowen Terrace to Kangaroo Point having served as a red herring dragged across the trail to divert attention. Discussion on this scheme waxes hot'. This 'red herring' is today's Story Bridge.

Story Bridge

The magnificent bridge spanning the river between Kangaroo Point and New Farm was originally referred to as the Jubilee Bridge to commemorate King George V's Silver Jubilee. The name was changed later to the Story Bridge in honour of J.D. Story, a former Public Service Commissioner, Vice-Chancellor of the University, a member of the Bridge Board and a keen advocate for the construction of the bridge.

The contract for the bridge was awarded on 30 April 1935 to Evans Deakin–Hornibrook Constructions Limited, a joint venture by two of the best names in the history of Brisbane's construction industry. The first sod was turned by the Premier of Queensland, W. Forgan Smith, on 24 May 1935. Designer of the bridge was J.J. Bradfield.

The difficult task of joining the bridge to complete it, and bringing each portion of the structure into the correct position, was effected by wedge mechanisms designed for lowering. The bridge gap was closed on 28 October 1939. There was calm weather with slight showers, and the operation began shortly after 5.00 a.m. and was completed around 7.30 a.m.

The impressive steel cantilever bridge (the largest in Australia) 31 m above water level and with a channel span of 282 m, was opened by the Governor of Queensland, Sir Leslie Orme Wilson, on 6 July 1940. As well as naming the Story Bridge, he named the Bradfield Highway (from Main Street, Kangaroo Point to Bowen Terrace) and Kemp Place (the area from the Bradfield Highway to Ann Street). The initial toll was soon abolished, and the Story Bridge remains one of the most important connections between the north and south sides of the Brisbane River.

The last structural gap in the Story Bridge was closed on 28 October 1939 by wedge mechanisms designed for lowering. The bridge has since become a symbol of Brisbane and is specially lit at night.

Koalas and kangaroos are among the several groups of Australian native animals that are a familiar sight at Lone Pine.

The fame of Lone Pine Sanctuary spread internationally during the Second World War.

Lone Pine

Joseph Clarkson arrived in Brisbane by ship from England on 16 July 1866. For a time he and his family stayed at Fortitude Valley, but in November 1866 they moved to 4.6 ha of land he had acquired at Fig Tree Pocket. Here the family farmed with varying results, using trial and error and trying such things as cotton, maize, pineapples and vegetables. The family members were community minded and made a significant contribution to the development of the surrounding areas.

Joseph Clarkson died in 1902 aged 84 years. The property was subsequently sold and the Lone Pine Sanctuary has now developed there. The name of Lone Pine came from a grand hoop pine tree which had been planted by the Clarksons in 1866 when their first home in Queensland was built nearby.

The property was acquired in the 1920s by C.A.M. Reid, a former Brisbane produce merchant and auctioneer, who had been familiar with the area as a child. He acquired two koalas, Jack and Jill, and subsequently a colony developed. Lone Pine also came to have kangaroos, wallabies, wallaroos, snakes, parrots and dingoes, as well as other Australian animals.

During the Second World War, the fame of the Lone Pine Sanctuary spread internationally through the number of Americans who visited there to view the strange Australian native animals. Mrs Douglas MacArthur is said to have visited Lone Pine on several occasions with her young son. Lone Pine is still a popular favourite with both visitors and locals.

Cumbooquepa (Somerville House)

In February 1942 during the Second World War, one of Brisbane's leading girls schools, Somerville House, was commandeered for use by the armed services — as were many of Brisbane's buildings.

Somerville House was originally a private residence, Cumbooquepa, erected c. 1890 for the family of Thomas Blacket Stephens, newspaper proprietor and businessman, Brisbane's second Mayor and a member of the Queensland Parliament for many years. *Cumbooquepa* is derived from an old local Aboriginal name for a group of waterholes nearby.

The building was designed by architect G.H.M. Addison to take full advantage of the magnificent site in Vulture Street, South Brisbane, overlooking the river and town. The long main facade, on public display, incorporated colonnades and arcading with intricate detail and massing, the red brick contrasting with pale detailing. Beneath an imposing polygonal tower, a central entrance porch led to a main vestibule featuring four long stained glass windows magnificently depicting Shakespearean characters. This, in turn, led to an outstanding interior with hand carved joinery, ornamental fireplaces, leaded windows, and a vaulted ceiling to a magnificent dining-room.

In December 1919, the Presbyterian and Methodist Schools Association acquired Cumbooquepa for use by the Brisbane High School for Girls. The name Somerville House was bestowed to honour Mary Somerville, mathematician and physical scientist, who significantly furthered the cause of higher education for women.

During the war, Somerville House was used as the Headquarters of the United States Army East Asian Command. The school was relocated, air raid slit trenches were constructed in the school grounds and the splendid stained glass windows were removed and stored, being replaced when the army vacated Somerville House. The school also returned after the war.

In 1986, Old Girls of the school rallied from around the country in protest against an offer to the School Council from an overseas syndicate to buy the school as a trade centre (adjoining the Expo 88 site). With the final rejection of the offer, the historic traditions and heritage of Somerville House were upheld.

Built as a residence c. 1890, Cumbooquepa became a leading girls school, Somerville House, in January 1920. Its four magnificent stained glass panels, depicting Shakespearean characters, were removed for the duration of the occupation by the American Forces in the Second World War, and were later reinstated.

American War Memorial, Newstead Park

The first convoy of Americans to arrive in Brisbane during the Second World War reached here on 22 December 1941. Brisbane subsequently became the base for hundreds of thousands of American servicemen in the Pacific during the most critical part of the War and was the centre from which vast forces were deployed in campaigns leading to ultimate victory in the cause of freedom.

It was only five months after the arrival of the first Americans that the joint Australian–American naval and air victory in the Coral Sea Battle was effected — a most significant event in the safety and history of Australia. This Battle 'marked the nearest approach of hostile forces in strength to the coastline of Australia and our deliverance from threatened invasion'. The Battle was subsequently commemorated throughout Australia each year by Coral Sea Week. One of the highlights of the tenth anniversary in Brisbane was the unveiling on 3 May 1952 of the stone memorial erected in Newstead Park, commemorating the American contribution to the defence of Australia during the Second World War.

The memorial is surmounted by a 1.5 m emblematic eagle of the United States and stands 10.6 m high from the pavement to the top of the eagle. The column beneath the eagle is 1 m in diameter. The memorial, constructed mainly of Helidon freestone and with a base of Queensland axed granite, is flanked by two flag poles each 7.6 m high. The memorial's inscription reads:—

> This monument was erected by the people of Queensland in grateful memory of the contribution made by the people of the United States of America to the defence of this country during the 1939–45 war. Long may it stand as a symbol of the unity of English speaking peoples in the cause of freedom.

> The Australian–American Association initiated and implemented the erection of this Memorial. The funds were raised by Public Appeal launched by the Lord Mayor of Brisbane on 3rd March, 1950. The first sod was turned by the President of the Association on 3rd May, 1951, in the presence of the Premier of Queensland and the Ambassador Extraordinary and Minister Plenipotentiary of the United States of America.

The emblematic eagle of the United States surmounts the memorial in Newstead Park commemorating America's contribution to the defence of Australia during the Second World War.

MacArthur Chambers

During the Second World War, one of Brisbane's Queen Street buildings became the General Headquarters — South West Pacific Area, which contained the office of the Commander-in-Chief, General Douglas MacArthur. The building had opened on 2 March 1934 as the Australian Mutual Provident Society's head office in Queensland and it was the Society's Board Room on the eighth floor which became MacArthur's office.

By 30 June 1942 the Hiring Department of the Defence Forces had taken over the entire second to ninth floors and tenants were compulsorily evacuated under orders from the military authorities. It was during MacArthur's occupancy of this building that the plans which won the war in this theatre were developed.

During the Second World War a 'Brisbane Line' strategy existed whereby, if necessary, Australia's defence was to be concentrated within a line running from Brisbane to Melbourne. In 1942, army leaders were advised that, subject to contrary direction from the government, North Queensland and Tasmania should not be reinforced, and General MacArthur's plans for the defence of Australia also included abandoning the north and the west. From late in 1942 however, Australia's strategic position improved and the 'Brisbane Line' became a non-issue strategically though not politically.

The former A.M.P. building is now called MacArthur Chambers to perpetuate the memory of its war-time associations with this famous figure and what he represented.

MacArthur Chambers (Left) is named in honour of General Douglas MacArthur (Above, Right) and his historic associations with the building.

The main entrance to the original building of the University of Queensland at St Lucia.

University of Queensland, St Lucia

The University's accommodation at the Old Government House site very soon proved inadequate and in 1926 the Senate accepted the offer by Dr James O'Neil Mayne and his sister Mary to meet the cost of acquisition of some 90 ha of riverside land at St Lucia. However, it wasn't until 6 March 1937 that the foundation stone was laid. Architects were Hennessy, Hennessy and Co. and the initial building programme was to include the Main Building, the Chemistry Building and the Geology Building. Helidon free-stone, Greymere and Samford granite and Brisbane bricks were used as construction materials.

Work was suspended in 1942 due to the Second World War, but the buildings were sufficiently advanced for occupation from 1 August 1942 to 31 December 1944 as the Advance Headquarters of Sir Thomas Blaimey, Commander-in-Chief of the Australian Military Forces and Commander of the Allied Land Forces in the South West Pacific Area. Work resumed in 1945 and in 1949 the library and various departments within the Arts Faculty moved to St Lucia. By 1950 'the centre of gravity had changed clearly from George Street to St Lucia'.

These original buildings were designed to form a circle, and arcaded cloisters on the inner circumference surround a magnificent Great Court. Column capitals are carved with the coats of arms and crests of the principal universities of the world and gargoyles are carved in the stone walls above. The facades, especially to the main entrances and tower, also carry interesting carvings including historic events in Queensland, the State's flora and fauna, representations of Aboriginal social life and customs, the founding of the University and the establishment of the University at St Lucia. Many buildings have been constructed and other developments have occurred over the years, and the original benefactors who made the University's existence at St Lucia possible are commemorated in one of the more recent buildings, the Mayne Hall.

A recent view of Moorlands, former home of the University benefactors Dr James Mayne and his sister Mary.

Moorlands

Moorlands was the home of the Mayne family and on the deaths of Dr James Mayne and Miss Mary Mayne in 1939 and 1940 respectively, Moorlands was bequeathed to the University of Queensland. This institution's St Lucia site and the Veterinary School site at Moggill had already been acquired through the generosity of these two people.

It is understood that Moorlands was built sometime between 1878 and 1882 by Mrs Mary Mayne, mother of the University benefactors and widow of Patrick Mayne, a Queen Street butcher who, at his death in 1865, owned much valuable property throughout Queensland. Mrs Mayne died in the early 1890s and of her children, one daughter entered a convent and two sons died by the early

1900s. Thus Moorlands and the other properties of the estate passed to the eligible children, Mary and James.

This magnificent Victorian home was sold by the University in 1945 to the Brisbane Legacy War Widows and Orphans Fund as a home for war orphaned children and war widows. In 1971 the property was sold again to the Methodist Church, which built the Wesley Hospital at the rear of the Moorlands grounds. The old residence was occupied by the Blue Nursing Service State Council, who have restored the exterior and recycled the interior as offices. Patients in the Wesley Hospital are now able to view the Brisbane River across this grand old home with its formal garden of magnificent mature Bunya pines, jacaranda and poinciana trees.

A view from the Executive Building in William Street across the central city area to Kangaroo Point, on Tuesday, 29 January 1974. Mary Street is at the extreme left, Alice Street is at the extreme right and Margaret Street is angled across the centre of the picture.

A view in the opposite direction across the Brisbane River to the flooded South Brisbane area.

The 1974 Flood

When Brisbane people woke to a depressingly rainy and blustery day on Friday, 25 January 1974, they little realised that the following weekend would bring such anguish and devastation to the capital, caused by the worst floods in Brisbane since 1893. The weekend was a long weekend, with a public holiday on the Monday for the official celebration of Australia Day — the anniversary of the foundation of British settlement in Australia on 26 January 1788. But this was not to be a weekend of celebration, though it was certainly one to remember.

Cyclone Wanda crossed the Queensland coast at Double Island Point on Thursday evening, 24 January 1974, and the monsoonal trough brought south by it caused very heavy rainfalls over the next few days, with Brisbane city receiving 642.6 mm to 9.00 a.m. on Saturday.

Major flooding occurred in Brisbane's creeks and of the 3 flash floods, the second was the highest ever recorded, with several houses being swept away.

In the Brisbane city area the first minor flooding on the river occurred at high tide about midday on Friday, when the tides were higher than normal and the river contained flood run off from the metropolitan creeks.

Flood run off from the Bremer River at Ipswich caused sharp rises in the Brisbane River and at 1.00 a.m. on Sunday a height of 4.3 m was recorded at the Brisbane Port Office. River levels continued to rise, reaching a peak of 6.6 m at 2.15 a.m. on Tuesday, 29 January. The Brisbane River on this day was more than 3 km wide in some areas. That afternoon Brisbane's Lord Mayor ordered releases from the Somerset Dam stopped, to allow the Brisbane River to fall and the floodwaters to clear as quickly as possible.

By 5.00 a.m. on Wednesday, 30 January, the river height had fallen to 5.6 m and continued to fall. By Thursday, 31 January, flooding had eased in the city reaches and that afternoon the flood gates at Somerset Dam were opened again to prevent the backed up water flooding the township of Kilcoy.

As the floodwaters had continued to rise unbelievably, houses were swept away, possessions were lost forever, and people were heartbroken. In Brisbane, 13 750 houses were affected; in neighbouring Ipswich, 4 000 houses were damaged or destroyed; and flood deaths in these areas totalled 15.

Subsequently, the receding waters revealed a scene of chaos and devastation. But the Brisbane community responded with help in the cleaning-up process, amid the debris and mud deposited as the raging torrent once again became the familiar, calm and majestic Brisbane River, meandering through the city on its way to Moreton Bay.

The heartbreaking aftermath of the 1974 Flood — a house that is no longer a home.

The Regatta Hotel at Toowong has always been well maintained and has recently undergone minor restoration.

A group of recently restored cottages in Cairns Street, Kangaroo Point.

Restoration and Recycling of Old Buildings

During the 1970s there was a vast upsurge of national pride in Australia's past and with this came a new-found appreciation of old buildings.

Concurrent with this feeling and an ever increasing demand for housing, came the realisation that often it could be cheaper and easier, as well as more rewarding, to 'do up an old place' rather than build or buy a new house. The result has been an increasing number of restored homes — from humble cottages to larger residences.

Two adjacent groups of run-down terrace houses in Petrie Terrace were recently renovated and recycled as restaurants.

In some cases, as in the older suburbs of Petrie Terrace, Spring Hill and Kangaroo Point, groups of houses have been restored either by the individual owner/occupiers or by a speculative owner. The results have inspired many others to embark on similar ventures and a trend has now ensued.

Many buildings such as hotels, business and commercial premises, have had their exteriors restored to their former glory whilst their interiors have been completely or partially modernised for the same or an alternate use. Several larger buildings, including churches, warehouses and residences,

have been converted for reuse for alternate purposes such as restaurants, art galleries and community centres. Buildings recycled as restaurants, for example, include a former church (St Luke's) used for some years as Brisbane's Anglican Cathedral, two adjacent groups of two storey terrace houses in Petrie Terrace, and several former residences.

As a consequence of this recycling trend, an increasing number of old buildings which previously would have been demolished are now being retained and their charm is being recaptured through restoration.

Moving House

In recent years many of the older residences have been threatened with demolition for redevelopment of the site, generally for modern home units, and in traditional Queensland style the more fortunate of these homes have been transported to new sites where they have been re-erected and restored. One area of Brisbane where, for example, the 'transportable houses' have been re-erected and restored is at Pullenvale. The sites are generally large and are ideal as a setting for these spacious old homes, which are usually the ones chosen as 'worth saving' by 'moving house'.

The materials and methods of construction of Queensland houses make them particularly suitable for removal from one site to another. When the Toowong site of this fine house was to be redeveloped, the house was transported in sections (Above) to a new site at Pullenvale. Here it was carefully and lovingly restored to its former glory (Right) and its splendid architecture continues to provide enjoyment for the viewer.

The City Square. The historic Albert Street Uniting Church contrasts with the S.G.I.O. Building rising behind it; the M.I.M. Building, the Ann Street Presbyterian Church and the Reserve Bank of Australia (to the right, not pictured) overlook the Square.

City Square and Uniting Church

The original King George Square, overlooked by the City Hall, was reconstructed during the 1970s and traffic which formerly passed along Albert Street and through the square was rerouted. The square was redesigned and its level raised to accommodate the King George Square Car Park below.

Overlooking the square like sentinels are the Albert Street Uniting Church and, towering above it and forming a backdrop to it, the State Government Insurance Building, officially opened on 28 October 1970.

The Albert Street Uniting Church was built originally as the Albert Street Methodist Church and was opened on 8 November 1889 by Lady Norman, wife of the Governor, Sir Henry Wylie Norman. Architects were Oakden Addison and Kemp, and the red brick building with Oamaru stone relief was lit internally by some fine stained glass windows executed by the well known Brisbane firm of Exton and Gough. The church was designed in the 'decorated Gothic style of architecture — a style very much favoured by the Wesleyan body in other colonies' and an attempt was made to 'meet some of the inconveniences which a sub-tropical climate like ours entail. The building is surrounded by enclosed cloisters, which are designed to shade the walls from the sun, and to keep the interior of the building cool. This system adds considerably to the appearance of the building'.

The modern Parliamentary Annexe rises into the evening sky, dwarfing the original Parliament House beside it.

Parliamentary Annexe

Opened in March 1979 by the Duke of Gloucester, this modern 24-level adjunct to the fine old Parliament House building rises panoramically above the Brisbane River and houses the 82 members of Parliament during the renovation of the old building. The Annexe presently provides accommodation for the Legislative Assembly Chamber, Parliamentary Library, offices and recreational facilities, as well as living quarters for ministers and for country members, previously housed in the now demolished Bellevue Hotel opposite the old Parliament House.

Only the best materials were used for the construction of the building and for its furniture and furnishings. Such materials include oak, blackbean, red cedar and imported Italian marble, imported Waterford and Stuart crystal drinking vessels and Royal Doulton crockery embossed with the Queensland emblem. A large bronze by well known local husband and wife artists, Leonard and Kathleen Shillam, hangs in the entrance hall. It depicts the State Coat of Arms granted to Queensland by the Royal College of Heralds and presented during the visit of Her Majesty Queen Elizabeth II to Brisbane in 1977.

The entrance and walls around the new Parliamentary Annexe were built by the same family firm of Andrew Petrie Pty Ltd, which constructed the original Parliament House building in George Street in the 1860s.

The elegance of the third permanent Victoria Bridge is captured in this evening view from South Brisbane. Some pylons of the previous bridge are still visible in the background.

Victoria Bridge and Memorial

The Victoria Bridge which opened in 1897 was replaced by a sleek modern counterpart during the 1960s. The new bridge, 313 m long, was completed in January 1969 at a cost of $2 300 000, met equally by the State Government and the Brisbane City Council. The design of the bridge was carried out by the Coordinator General's Department.

The new Victoria Bridge was built adjacent to and on the western side of the old bridge, which was then demolished. Initially, however, both bridges were used together, outbound traffic using two lanes of the old bridge and inbound traffic two lanes of the new bridge. This coincided with the conversion of Brisbane's public transport system from trams to buses.

During the demolition of the old bridge a box was found in stonework at the Queen Street end, which contained ten coins, a medal and old clippings from the *Brisbane Courier* reporting the opening of the bridge on 22 June 1897. The medal was issued by the Municipality of Brisbane to commemorate the sixtieth year of Queen Victoria's reign in 1897.

One southern entrance to the old bridge was retained and included two sets of the old tram tracks as well as some stonework from the first permanent Victoria Bridge in its base. The archway carried a memorial plaque to an eleven-year-old Greek boy, Hector Vasyli, who was killed on 9 June 1918 by a vehicle carrying returned soldiers whom he was welcoming home. The Returned Services League, the Hellenic Association and Brisbane citizens erected the plaque on the bridge near the site of the accident and since then a wreath has been placed at the memorial each Anzac Day.

The old stone arch today also stands as 'a memorial to the endeavour of successive generations of Brisbane citizens to provide a swift means of cross river transport'.

The arch at the southern entrance to the second permanent Victoria Bridge was retained as a monument when the bridge was demolished.

124

Queensland Railways' 'missing link'. The Merivale Bridge joined the southern suburban railway system with other Queensland railway systems at Roma Street station. The new bridge harmonizes with the graceful lines of the earlier William Jolly Bridge, one of several cross-river road bridges.

Cross River Rail Link

'One of the curious sights of Brisbane is the stream of people walking over the water from south to north in the mornings and back again in the afternoons. They do so by the Victoria Bridge'. Thus commented Peter Trundle in the *Courier-Mail* of 8 November 1978. The reason for this curiosity was the lack of a railway bridge connecting the northern and southern sides of the city — southerners disembarked at South Brisbane and walked across the bridge to work in the city.

There had been agitation for a cross river rail link as early as the 1880s but it was not until Saturday, 18 November 1978 that the idea became a reality when the Merivale Bridge was officially opened by the Premier of Queensland, Joh Bjelke-Petersen. The project had been given the go-ahead by

State Cabinet in October 1971 and the bridge, designed by Cameron, McNamara and Partners, was begun in August 1975. The bridge was designed to carry both narrow and standard gauge tracks, the latter not laid initially, and South Brisbane remained the terminus of the interstate trains for some time. The link between the northern and southern Brisbane suburban rail systems cost over $20,000,000 and patronage has shown that this expenditure was amply justified.

In 1980 the Merivale Bridge was named the year's most outstanding engineering project, winning top honours in the awards of the Association of Consulting Engineers, Australia. 'Careful consideration was given to aesthetics and the environment and it was functional, economic and pleasing in appearance'. The bridge also won the 1979 Steel Award.

Mount Coot-tha Botanic Gardens

The foothills of the Mount Coot-tha Forest Park Reserve, on the eastern slopes of the Taylor Range, were selected by the Brisbane City Council as the site for a new Botanic Gardens — the old Brisbane Botanic Gardens, established in the city in the 1850s, allowed no further room for expansion. The new gardens opened in 1976 and today attract about half a million people annually. They feature examples of such widely diverse micro-climates as tropical rain forest, desert, tropical wet, tropical dry, lagoon and marsh.

Above: *General view at the new Botanical Gardens at Mount Coot-tha, showing the Sir Thomas Brisbane Planetarium.*

Opposite: *The tropical plant display dome seen from one of the many walkways in the new Gardens.*

126

A tropical plant display dome opened in December 1977 is an eye-catching, space-age structure providing a carefully controlled environment in an enormous transparent, smoke-tinted acrylic bubble with an aluminium alloy frame. It is 28 m in diameter and 9 m high inside, with a centre-piece formed by a circular pool 12 m in diameter.

The Sir Thomas Brisbane Planetarium opened in 1978 and its Star Theatre has seats which rotate through 60°, allowing the occupants to view a full compass span of simulated sky projected onto a giant screen provided by the specially constructed interior of the 12.5 m dome. Sir Thomas Brisbane not only was responsible for the founding of Brisbane, but also was responsible for the setting up of the first observatory at Parramatta, near Sydney, after his arrival as Governor of New South Wales in 1821. Observations carried out here from 1822 to 1826 led to his catalogue of stars.

The beautiful and informative gardens developed at Mount Coot-tha have attracted many birds to the area and it is here that man, bird and plant can come together in one of Australia's most pleasant environments.

A model of the completed Queensland Cultural Centre on the south bank of the Brisbane River.

The interior of the Queensland Art Gallery, showing the Water Mall.

Queensland Cultural Centre

Moves in the late 1960s to build a new Queensland Art Gallery culminated in the early 1970s with a grand vision for a cultural centre, to accommodate art, music, dance, theatre, literature, history and science at one readily accessible and versatile venue.

The Queensland Art Gallery, opened in 1982, was the first stage of the Queensland Cultural Centre designed by Robin Gibson. It is one of the most modern, up to date and exciting galleries in the world. A water mall with dramatic fountains and water sculptures, an outdoor sculpture area and gardens,

The Queensland Art Gallery at dusk. Opened on 21 June 1982, the Gallery was the first stage of the Queensland Cultural Centre.

and 4700 square metres of viewing space with various ceiling heights, are only some of the Gallery's distinctive features. Walkways link the Gallery with other parts of the Cultural Centre.

The Performing Arts Centre, Stage II of the Cultural Centre, opened in 1905. A Lyric Theatre and a Concert Hall, for both visiting and local productions, are the main components. The theatre provides for audiences of varing capacity — 1000, 1500 or 2000. The classic Concert Hall includes a German designed, modernistic, 6500 pipe organ, catering to a variety of musical talents from classical to jazz. A smaller Cremorne Theatre allows for experimentation.

The Queensland Museum opened as Stage III of the Centre in 1986. Its 6500 square metres of floor space accommodates displays of the Museum's collections, which represent the natural, human, and technological history of Queensland. A geomorphic garden contains educational displays.

The State Library completed the complex in 1988. Its reading room on three levels and landscaped balconies capture the fine views of the river and city, and a skylit three-storeyed atrium suffuses the exhibition spaces and marble paved entrance with natural light. The John Oxley Library, also included in the new building, provides the opportunity to explore Queensland's history in its many aspects.

An auditorium and restaurant, also included in the Centre, overlook landscaped terraces to the river.

Griffith University

Initially conceived as an adjunct to the University of Queensland to relieve pressure in the humanities, Griffith University opened at Nathan as an autonomous institution in 1975. It is named after Sir Samuel Griffith, former Premier and Chief Justice of Queensland and the first Chief Justice of the High Court of Australia.

The site of the University is truly Australian, set on a sandstone hill amongst the natural flora which includes the envied 'blackboys'. The buildings have been designed to complement the site and to cope with the local subtropical climate, incorporating architectual means of cooling such as deep overhangs and through draughts.

The accommodation village at Griffith University housed the athletes attending the XII Commonwealth Games in Brisbane in 1982. The Queen Elizabeth II Jubilee Sport Centre, a venue for the Games, is within walking distance of the village.

Buildings at Griffith University are set amongst native flora which forms an integral part of the campus.

The 'hub' building, at the centre of Griffith University's accommodation village, was used by athletes attending the XII Commonwealth Games in 1982.

Gateway Bridge

A gala carnival celebrated the opening of the Gateway Bridge on Saturday 11 January 1986, with an estimated 200,000 people participating from 6.00 a.m. — the only occasion when pedestrians have been permitted on the bridge. It opened to vehicular traffic the following morning.

The main river span — a 260 metre concrete box girder — is 65 metres above the Brisbane River at its highest point, and is believed to have been the longest of its type in the world at the time of its construction. The bridge links the Gold and Sunshine coasts highways, helping to alleviate some of Brisbane's traffic problems.

Situated towards the mouth of the Brisbane River, close to Brisbane Airport, the Gateway Bridge marks the entrance to Brisbane for most visitors, whether they are travelling by land, sea or air.

The majestic Gateway Bridge, 65 metres above the Brisbane River at its highest point and located close to Brisbane Airport and the river mouth, indicates the entrance to Brisbane for many visitors.

A model of World Expo superimposed on the 40 hectare site at South Brisbane (centre left), just 800 metres from Brisbane's city heart on the north side of the river.

World Expo 88

The international tradition of World Expositions (Expo) began with the London Exposition of 1851, when twenty-five countries participated. Since then, twenty-one World Expos have been held in cities throughout the world. An Expo is a world fair, where nations gather 'to review and predict man's cultural and technological evolution through exhibitions and performances'. World Expos are controlled by the Bureau of International Expositions under a convention signed in Paris in 1928. Participation by countries is invited through diplomatic channels.

World Expo 88 is being held in Brisbane — the first Expo in the Southern Hemisphere since 1888 — and is the highlight of Australia's Bicentenary. The theme is 'Leisure in the Age of Technology', and fifty-two governments are participating.

The 40 hectare site on the south bank of the Brisbane River, only 800 metres from the city heart, provides 60,000 square metres of exhibit space. Temporary international pavilions are decorated by the exhibitors. The most distinctive feature of the site is its eye-catching canopy of huge PVC-coated polyester umbrellas — 'sun sails' — to help shade and otherwise protect visitors.

A 5 hectare, high technology amusement park, Australia's largest, features space oriented rides, exhibits and amusements; a river stage, with riverside seating for 12,000

provides a venue for concerts and national day celebrations; and there is an aquacade featuring high diving towers and diving wells for special events.

Also on site are some historic buildings surviving from the days when this area was a leading commercial and business district, with Stanley Street in South Brisbane closely rivalling Queen Street on the north side of the river. Historic buildings reused for Expo include two former hotels, a bank, a school of arts and library, a technical college, an art gallery and a concert hall.

The Expo site was one of the earliest areas developed in Brisbane: most of South Brisbane was cleared and sown to supply grain for the convict settlement. A road led from a ferry here to the Ipswich outstation (and subsequently further west), and the first south-side land sales were in this locality. Later, trams and an early railway ran through the area (a railway cutting survives near the former library), and extensive wharves lined the river.

These living components of South Brisbane's heritage integrate well with other structures on the site and are a fitting Australian cultural contribution to World Expo 88.

Stanley Street, South Brisbane, the site of World Expo 88, viewed from the direction of the Victoria Bridge during the 1893 flood.

Top left: *Dating probably from the early 1870s, the Ship Inn served the shipping trade from the dry dock opposite and the extensive wharves lining the south bank of the river. It also served travellers passing to and from the south and west, being the southernmost hotel in Stanley Street. In a run-down condition by the early 1980s, the old building was renovated, enlarged and computerised in keeping with the theme of World Expo 88. The Ship Inn forms a historic precinct with the former Dry Dock, Municipal Library, Town Hall, Cumbooquepa and Soldiers Memorial Park.*

Above left: *Built in Stanley Street in 1885, the Plough Inn was described in 1888 as 'one of the principal hotels on this street, very conveniently situated, and is frequented by persons engaged in the shipping interest and a goodly number of sporting fraternity'. The decorative parapet and cast iron lace contrast with the more restrained timber decoration of the Ship Inn.*

Top right: *Constructed in 1885 for drapers Allan and Stark (later Myers), this decorative Victorian building housed a branch of the Queensland National Bank (now National Australia) from 1888 to 1943, and the South Brisbane Gas and Light Company (later Allgas Energy Ltd) from 1897 to 1985. Re-opening for Expo as Central House, the building again accommodates a bank — Westpac's Expo headquarters — as well as other facilities.*

Above right: *The old South Brisbane Municipal Library, comprising three main sections (the earliest probably predating 1882), is a building of multifarious uses: former Post and Telegraph Office, School of Arts, Technical College, Art Gallery, City Concert Hall and Library; Convention Centre and Bulletin Executive Club during World Expo 88; and, after Expo, the State Headquarters of the Queensland Surf Lifesaving Association.*

Index

'Old buildings do not belong to us only; they belonged to our forefathers and they will belong to our descendants unless we play them false. They are not in any sense our property to do as we like with them. We are only trustees for those who come after us'.

William Morris.